ALL ABOUT THE

USA

A CULTURAL READER

MILADA BROUKAL

PETER MURPHY

Longman

All About the USA: A Cultural Reader

Longman, 10 Bank Street, White Plains, N.Y. 10606

Associated companies:
Longman Group Ltd., London
Longman Cheshire Pty., Melbourne
Longman Paul Pty., Auckland
Copp Clark Pitman, Toronto

Special thanks to Randee Falk for her contribution to the readings.

Photo credits: Page 10, From the Collections of Henry Ford Museum &
Greenfield Village; page 22, Mark Twain Memorial, Hartford, CT; page 31,
Photo provided courtesy of Washington, DC Convention and Visitors
Association; page 37, National Park Service Photo; page 40, N.Y. Conven-
tion & Visitors Bureau; page 46, Courtesy of The Duffle Bag, Carmel, NY,
10512; page 55, The Noah Webster Foundation and Historical Society of
West Hartford, CT, Inc.; page 67, National Park Service Photo; page 73,
The Stowe-Day Foundation, Hartford, CT; page 79, Courtesy of the New
York Historical Society, New York City; page 88, AP/Wide World Photos.

Distributed in the United Kingdom by Longman Group
Ltd., Longman House, Burnt Mill, Harlow, Essex CM2O
2JE, England and by associated companies, branches,
and representatives throughout the world.

Executive editor: Joanne Dresner
Development editor: Debbie Sistino
Production editor: Janice L. Baillie
Text design: Pencil Point Studio
Cover design: Susan J. Moore
Cover photos: Top row, left to right: Library of Congress, Courtesy of
    Minneapolis Convention Bureau, Canadian Government Office of Tourism;
    center row, left to right: Greater New Orleans Tourist & Convention
    Commission, Inc., Library of Congress, Mary Anne Fackelman/The White
    House; bottom row, left to right: Courtesy of the Ford Archives, Dearborn,
    Michigan, The Port Authority of NY & NJ, Library of Congress
Text art: Pencil Point Studio: Terry Kovalcik, Donna Ruff, Tom Sperling
Photo research: Polli Heyden
Production supervisor: Kathleen M. Ryan

Library of Congress Cataloging in Publication Data

Broukal, Milada.
    All about the USA : a cultural reader / Milada Broukal, Peter
Murphy.
        p.   cm.
    ISBN 0-8013-0637-X
    1. Readers—United States.   2. English language—Textbooks for
foreign speakers.   3. United States—Civilization.   I. Murphy,
Peter, 1947–   .   II. Title.
PE1127.H5B68   1991
428.6'4—dc20   90-47057
                                                              CIP

CONTENTS

INTRODUCTION

All about the USA is a low-intermediate reader for students of English as a Second Language. Thirty units introduce typically American people, places, and things. A host of facts presented in the units will not only provide students with information about the USA, but will also stimulate cross-cultural exchange. The vocabulary and structures used in the text have been carefully controlled at an intermediate level, while every effort has been made to keep the language natural.

Each unit contains:

- Prereading questions and introductory visuals
- A short reading passage
- Topic-related vocabulary work
- Comprehension of main ideas
- Comprehension of details
- Grammar
- Discussion questions

The prereading questions are linked to the visual on the first page of each unit. They focus the students on the topic of the unit by introducing names, encouraging speculation about content, involving the students' own experience when possible, and presenting vocabulary as the need arises.

The reading of each passage should, ideally, first be done individually by skimming for a general feel for content. The teacher may wish to deal with some of the vocabulary at this point. A second, more detailed individual reading could be done while working through the vocabulary exercise. Further reading(s) could be done aloud by the teacher or with the class.

The VOCABULARY exercise is designed to help students become more self-reliant by encouraging them to work out meaning from context. As suggested previously, this section can be done during the reading phase or afterwards or both. As in all exercise sections, a variety of exercise types is used.

There are two COMPREHENSION exercises: *Looking for Main Ideas* should be used in conjunction with the text to help students develop their reading skills, and not as a test of memory. In each case, the students are asked to confirm the basic content of the text, which they can do either individually, in pairs, in small groups, or as a whole class. *Looking for Details* expands the students' exploration of the text, concentrating on the skimming and scanning skills necessary to derive maximum value from reading.

GRAMMAR focuses on aspects of the language suggested by the reading passage itself. The emphasis is on practice and reinforcement rather than teaching, while indirectly building on the comprehension phase.

DISCUSSION gives the students the opportunity to bring their own knowledge and imagination to the topics and related areas. They may wish to discuss all of the questions in their small groups or to select one on which to report back to the class.

THE HOT DOG

What do you see in the picture?
What kind of dog is it?
Do you like hot dogs?

In its home country of Germany, the hot dog was called the *frankfurter*. It was named after Frankfurt, a German city.

Frankfurters were first sold in the United States in the 1860s. Americans called frankfurters "dachshund sausages." A dachshund is a dog from Germany with a very long body and short legs. "Dachshund sausage" seemed like a good name for the frankfurter.

Dachshund sausages first became popular in New York, especially at baseball games. At games they were sold by men who kept them warm in hot-water tanks. As the men walked up and down the rows of people, they yelled, "Get your dachshund sausages! Get your hot dachshund sausages!" People got the sausages on buns, a special bread.

One day in 1906 a newspaper cartoonist named Tad Dorgan went to a baseball game. When he saw the men with the dachshund sausages, he got an idea for a cartoon. The next day at the newspaper office he drew a bun with a dachshund inside—not a dachshund sausage, but a dachshund. Dorgan didn't know how to spell *dachshund*. Under the cartoon, he wrote "Get your hot dogs!"

The cartoon was a sensation, and so was the new name. If you go to a baseball game today, you can still see sellers walking around with hot-water tanks. As they walk up and down the rows they yell, "Get your hot dogs here! Get your hot dogs!"

VOCABULARY

Complete the definitions. Circle the letter of the correct answer.

1. The special bread used for a hot dog is a _____ .
   a. sausage   **b.** bun   **c.** dachshund

2. Another word for *to shout* is to _____ .
   a. name   **b.** draw   **c.** yell

3. A line of objects or people is a _____ .
   a. row   **b.** game   **c.** cartoon

4. When something is a cause of excitement, it is _____ .
   a. an idea   **b.** a sensation   **c.** a hot dog

5. Large containers for water or other liquids, sometimes made of metal, are called _____ .
   a. tanks   **b.** sellers   **c.** cartoonists

6. A funny drawing is a _____ .
   a. cartoonist   **b.** frankfurter   **c.** cartoon

COMPREHENSION

A. Looking for Main Ideas

Write the questions for these answers.

1. What _____ ?
   Americans called frankfurters "dachshund sausages."

2. Where _____ ?
   Dachshund sausages were first sold at baseball games.

3. Who _____ ?
   Tad Dorgan was a newspaper cartoonist.

B. Looking for Details

Circle T if the sentence is true. Circle F if the sentence is false.

	True	False
1. Frankfurters were first sold in the United States in the 1960s.	T	F
2. A dachshund is a dog with a long body and short legs.	T	F
3. At baseball games today you cannot see sellers walking around with hot-water tanks.	T	F

4. Tad Dorgan got an idea for a cartoon in his office.   T   F

5. Tad Dorgan drew a bun with a sausage inside.   T   F

6. The words under Tad Dorgan's cartoon were "Get your hot dogs!"   T   F

GRAMMAR

Complete the sentences using the past tense form of the verbs in parentheses.

EXAMPLE: Americans ___*called*___ frankfurters "dachshund sausages."
(call)

1. Dachshund sausages first _____ popular in New York.
(become)

2. The sellers _____ the sausages warm in hot-water tanks.
(keep)

3. People _____ the sausages on buns.
(get)

4. One day Tad Dorgan _____ to a baseball game.
(go)

5. He _____ the men with the dachshund sausages.
(see)

6. He _____ , "Get your hot dogs!" under the cartoon.
(write)

DISCUSSION

Discuss the answers to these questions with your classmates.

1. Besides hot dogs, what are other popular foods in the United States? What are some popular foods in your country?
2. Are hot dogs healthy for you? Why or why not?
3. What are some healthy foods? What are some foods that are not so healthy?

THE PONY EXPRESS

Unit 2

What do you think the man in the picture is doing?

Why do you think he is riding so fast?

How is mail delivered today?

Around 1850 the United States began to grow rapidly. New land was added to the country. The discovery of gold in California brought thousands of settlers to the west coast. The United States had been about 1,000 miles from east to west. Suddenly it was about 3,000 miles wide.

The U.S. postal service had a big problem: How could the mail travel between the East and California?

The postal service had two solutions. Neither solution was very good. Either stagecoaches carried mail on the trails the settlers used, or the mail was taken by ship around the tip of South America. Either way, the trip took about a month. When the mail finally arrived, it was very old.

Then, in 1860, the Pony Express began. The Pony Express went from the state of Missouri to Sacramento, California. It had 400 horses, 80 riders, and 180 stations. The stations were about ten miles apart. Riders went as fast as twenty-five miles per hour from one station to the next. At each station a new horse would be ready. Within a minute the rider was off again. Each rider went seventy-five miles before passing the mail to the next rider. The mail was delivered within eight days!

The Pony Express riders faced many dangers. They had to cross rivers, mountains, and deserts. They had to travel throughout the night and in all kinds of weather. The riders could be attacked at any time by bandits or Indians. Yet only one rider died, and he died after he had delivered his letters. The mail was lost only once.

Around the same time that the Pony Express started, the telegraph was invented. In 1861 a telegraph line was built across the country. News that took eight days to reach California now took only one hour. What the riders could do in eight days, the telegraph could do in an hour. So, the Pony Express ended just eighteen months after it had begun.

VOCABULARY

Replace the underlined words in the sentences with the words below.

throughout	tip	rapidly	apart
solutions	faced	settlers	trails

1. Around 1850 the United States began to grow <u>quickly</u>.

2. The Pony Express stations were ten miles <u>from one to another</u>.

3. The Pony Express riders <u>met</u> many dangers.

4. With the discovery of gold, thousands of <u>people who wanted to stay</u> came to California.

5. Stagecoaches carried mail on <u>small roads</u> used by the settlers.

6. Ships went around the <u>end</u> of South America to get to California.

7. The Pony Express riders had to travel <u>during</u> the night in all kinds of weather.

8. The U.S. Postal Service had two <u>answers</u> to carrying mail from the East to California.

COMPREHENSION

A. Looking for Main Ideas

Circle the letter of the best answer.

1. The Pony Express started _____ .
   a. because the telegraph was invented
   b. because there were 400 horses
   c. because mail service was slow

2. The Pony Express riders _____ .
   a. died after they delivered the mail
   b. faced many dangers
   c. traveled from South America to California

3. The Pony Express ended _____ .
   a. after eight days
   b. before the telegraph was invented
   c. after eighteen months

B. Looking for Details

Circle T if the sentence is true. Circle F if the sentence is false.

	True	False
1. Before 1850 the United States was only 3,000 miles wide, from east to west.	T	F
2. The Pony Express ended after one and a half years.	T	F
3. Riders traveled at seventy-five miles per hour.	T	F
4. The Pony Express delivered the mail within eight days.	T	F
5. The Pony Express riders rode in all kinds of weather.	T	F
6. In 1861 the Pony Express built a telegraph line across the United States.	T	F

GRAMMAR

Complete the sentences with the prepositions below.

around	to	in	from	by	throughout	across

EXAMPLE: What the riders could do _____*in*_____ eight days the

telegraph could do _____*in*_____ an hour.

1. Gold was discovered _____ California.

2. Thousands of settlers came _____ the west coast.

3. After 1850 the United States was 3,000 miles _____ east

_____ west.

4. Mail was carried _____ ship _____ the tip of South America.

5. The Pony Express Riders rode _____ the night.

6. A telegraph line was built _____ the country.

DISCUSSION

Discuss the answers to these questions with your classmates.

1. What systems of mail service do you have in your country?
2. How do you think mail will be sent in the year 2050?
3. What is the most interesting piece of mail you have ever received?

BLUE JEANS

What are the two people in the picture doing?

What are they wearing?

Do you wear blue jeans?

Levi Strauss, a young immigrant from Germany, arrived in San Francisco in 1850. California was in the middle of the Gold Rush. Thousands of men were coming to California to dig for gold. And Levi Strauss came to sell canvas to these gold miners. Canvas is a heavy fabric. So Levi Strauss thought the miners could use the canvas for tents.

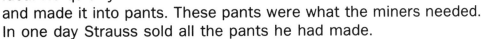

One day Strauss heard a miner complain that he couldn't find clothes strong enough for the work he was doing. Strauss got an idea. He quickly took some of his canvas and made it into pants. These pants were what the miners needed. In one day Strauss sold all the pants he had made.

Strauss wanted to improve his pants. He wanted to make them even better. He bought a fabric that was softer than canvas but just as strong. This fabric came from Nimes, a city in France, and was called *serge de Nimes*. The miners liked this fabric. They called it "denim" (from *de Nimes*) and bought even more pants from Strauss.

However, denim had no color. Because of this the denim pants did not look very interesting, and they got dirty easily. To solve these problems, Strauss dyed the denim blue.

Strauss continued to improve his jeans. Today, the company he started is known around the world. And jeans are considered not just practical but very fashionable as well.

VOCABULARY

What is the meaning of the underlined words? Circle the letter of the correct answer.

1. Strauss was a young underline{immigrant}.
   a. person who moves to another country
   b. person who is good in business

2. Canvas is a heavy underline{fabric}.
   a. machine
   b. cloth

3. The miners underline{complained} that they didn't have underline{strong clothes}.
   a. told about problems
   b. told stories

4. Strauss wanted to underline{improve} his pants.
   a. make them better
   b. make them cleaner

5. Strauss underline{dyed} the denim.
   a. changed the texture
   b. changed the color

6. Today, jeans are underline{considered} good for many uses.
   a. thought to be
   b. made to be

7. Blue jeans are underline{practical}.
   a. cheap
   b. useful

8. Blue jeans are underline{fashionable}.
   a. popular to wear
   b. interesting

COMPREHENSION

A. Looking for Main Ideas

Write complete answers to these questions.

1. Why did Levi Strauss come to California?

2. What did the miners need?

3. How did Strauss improve his pants?

B. Looking for Details

One word in each sentence is *not* correct. Cross out the word and write the correct answer above it.

1. Levi Strauss came to Germany in 1850.

2. There were thousands of men digging for canvas.

3. Levi Strauss came to buy canvas.

4. The miners needed clean pants.

5. Strauss made tents from denim.

6. Strauss got the denim from Germany.

7. Strauss dyed the denim red.

8. Levi jeans are known all over the United States.

GRAMMAR

Replace the underlined pronouns in the sentences with the correct nouns.

canvas	Miners	Levi Strauss	pants	the denim

1. <u>They</u> came to California for gold.

2. <u>He</u> came to California to sell canvas.

3. Miners used <u>it</u> to make tents.

4. Strauss used canvas to make <u>them</u>.

5. He dyed <u>it</u> blue.

6. Miners came to <u>him</u> to buy blue jeans.

DISCUSSION

Discuss the answers to these questions with your classmates.

1. Do you think Levi Strauss was a good businessman? Why or why not? Are you good in business?
2. If you could have your own business, what would it be?
3. What can clothes tell you about people?

HENRY FORD

Unit 4

Who is the man in the picture?

What is he doing?

Do you own a car?

Henry Ford was born in 1863 in the state of Michigan. He grew up on a farm but he did not want to become a farmer. He left school when he was sixteen. He wanted to make cars so he went to work as a mechanic.

In 1896 Ford built his first car. This car was very different from the cars of today. For example, its wheels were bicycle wheels.

In 1902 Ford built a car that won an important race. This car was the fastest car that had ever been built. It went seventy miles per hour. By then Ford had enough money to start the Ford Motor Company.

At this time cars cost a lot of money. Only very rich people bought cars. Ford had a dream. He wanted to build a car that many people could afford. Ford was sure that, if people could afford cars, they would buy them. He said, "everybody wants to be somewhere he isn't."

Ford's plan was to make all his cars the same. Cars that are all the same take less time and less money to make. Then Ford could charge less money for these cars. In 1908 Ford produced his famous Model T Ford. The Model T sold for $850. This was much cheaper than other cars but still more than most people could pay.

One day Ford visited a meat-packing factory. There he saw beef carcasses being moved from one worker to another. Each worker had a particular job to do when the beef carcasses reached him. Ford realized that he could use this assembly line method to build cars.

It took less than two hours to build a car on the assembly line. Before, it took fourteen hours. Ford was able to drop the price of the Model T to $265.

Ford's dream had come true. The Model T was now a car that many people could afford. By 1927, when Ford stopped making the Model T, over 15 million of these cars had been sold.

VOCABULARY

Which sentences have the same meaning as the sentences from the reading? Circle the letter of the correct answer.

1. Ford went to work as a mechanic.
   a. Ford fixed cars.
   b. Ford sold cars.

2. He wanted to build a car that many people could afford.
   a. He wanted to build a car many people would have enough money to buy.
   b. He wanted to build a car people would be able to sell easily.

3. He could charge less money for a car.
   a. He could ask people to use a credit card.
   b. He could ask people to pay less money.

4. Ford saw beef carcasses at the factory.
   a. Ford saw animals in boxes at the factory.
   b. Ford saw the bodies of dead animals at the factory.

5. Ford realized that he could use this assembly line method to build cars.
   a. Ford understood that the assembly line was a good way to build cars.
   b. Ford invented the assembly line equipment to build cars.

COMPREHENSION

A. Looking for Main Ideas

Circle the letter of the best answer.

1. Henry Ford built _____ .
   a. the first car
   b. the first bicycle
   c. a car with bicycle wheels

2. Henry Ford's dream was _____ .
   a. to build an assembly line
   b. to build a car most people could afford
   c. to build a car that would win a race

3. Ford first saw an assembly line _____ .
   a. at a meat-packing factory
   b. on a farm
   c. at the Ford Motor Company

B. Looking for Details

Circle T if the sentence is true. Circle F if the sentence is false.

	True	False
1. Henry Ford left school when he was sixteen.	T	F
2. Henry Ford made bicycle wheels on the farm.	T	F
3. Ford built a car that went seventy miles per hour.	T	F

	True	False
4. Only very poor people bought cars.	T	F
5. Ford said, "Everybody wants to be what he isn't."	T	F
6. The 1908 Model T cost more than most people could pay.	T	F
7. Before the assembly line it took fourteen hours to build two cars.	T	F
8. Ford dropped the price of the Model T by $585.	T	F

GRAMMAR

Complete the sentence using the past tense form of the verbs in parentheses.

EXAMPLE: Henry Ford's dream ___*came*___ true.
(come)

1. Ford _____ on a farm.
(grow up)

2. When he was sixteen, he _____ school.
(leave)

3. He _____ to work as a mechanic.
(go)

4. He _____ his first car in 1896.
(build)

5. Ford's 1902 car _____ an important race.
(win)

6. In those days, cars _____ a lot of money.
(cost)

7. Only very rich people _____ cars.
(buy)

8. The first Model T _____ for $850.
(sell)

DISCUSSION

Discuss the answers to these questions with your classmates.

1. Which car do you think is most popular in the United States?
2. What do you think the car of the future will look like?
3. There are more and more cars on the roads. What can be done to solve our traffic problems?

BASEBALL

What are the men in the picture doing?

Do you know how to play baseball?

Do you have a favorite baseball team?

Baseball is America's most popular sport. In a baseball game there are two teams of nine players. Players must hit a ball with a bat and then run around four bases. A player who goes around all the bases scores a run for his team. The team that finishes with more runs wins the game.

Where did baseball come from? No one knows for sure. Many people believe that the idea came from a game played by children in England. Other people believe that a man named Abner Doubleday invented the game in Cooperstown, New York, in 1839. But the first real rules of baseball were written in 1845 by Alexander Cartwright. Two teams from New York played a game following Cartwright's rules. The rules worked well. Soon there were many teams.

These early teams were not professional. They played only for fun, not money. But baseball was very popular from the start. Businessmen saw that they could make money with professional baseball teams.

The first professional team was started in 1869. This team was the Red Stockings of Cincinnati. Within a few years there were professional teams in other cities. In 1876 these teams came together in a league, or group, called the National League. The teams in the National League played one another.

In 1901 a new league, called the American League, was formed. To create some excitement, in 1903 the two leagues decided to have their first-place teams play each other. This event was called the World Series.

Each year since then the National League winner and the American League winner play in the World Series. And, each year, millions of people look forward to this exciting sports event.

VOCABULARY

Complete the definitions. Circle the letter of the correct answer.

1. A group of people that plays together is _____ .
   a. a team   **b.** a league   **c.** a game

2. A wooden stick used to hit a ball in baseball is called _____ .
   a. a ball   **b.** a sport   **c.** a bat

3. The four stations the players must go around are _____ .
   a. rules   **b.** bases   **c.** wins

4. When a player runs around all four bases he makes _____ .
   a. a four   **b.** a winner   **c.** a run

5. Teams that play a game the correct way are following the _____ .
   a. runs   **b.** rules   **c.** players

6. A group of sports teams is called _____ .
   a. first place teams   **b.** a league   **c.** a series

7. When something special or important happens it is _____ .
   a. an event   **b.** popular   **c.** a series

8. When teams play sports for money they are _____ .
   a. businessmen   **b.** fun   **c.** professional

COMPREHENSION

A. Looking for Main Ideas

Write the questions to these answers.

1. Where _____ ?
   No one knows where baseball came from. But the rules were written by Alexander Cartwright in 1845.

2. When _____ ?
   The first professional team started in 1869.

3. Who _____ ?
   The National League winner and the American League winner play in the World Series.

B. Looking for Details

Circle T if the sentence is true. Circle F if the sentence is false.

	True	False
1. Baseball was invented in England.	T	F
2. Abner Doubleday played the game with Alexander Cartwright.	T	F

	True	False
3. The early teams played for fun.	T	F
4. The Red Stockings were the first professional team.	T	F
5. In 1876 nonprofessional teams came together in a league.	T	F
6. The World Series has been played since 1903.	T	F
7. Baseball players must hit a ball with a bat and run around nine bases.	T	F
8. The first-place teams in each league play each other in the World Series.	T	F

GRAMMAR

Complete the sentences with the correct article. Use *a* or *the*. If no article is necessary, write X.

EXAMPLE: In __*a*__ baseball game there are __X__ two teams of nine players.

1. _____ baseball is _____ America's most popular sport.

2. Players must hit _____ ball with _____ bat.

3. No one knows where _____ baseball came from.

4. Some people believe that _____ man named Abner Doubleday

   invented _____ game in _____ New York.

5. _____ businessmen saw they could make _____ money with professional teams.

6. The teams in _____ National League played one another.

7. In 1901 _____ American League was formed.

8. _____ National League winner and _____ American League

   winner play each other in _____ World Series.

DISCUSSION

Discuss the answers to these questions with your classmates.

1. Baseball is the most popular sport in the United States. What is the most popular sport in your country?
2. Why do people play competitive sports? Do you play any sports? Which ones?
3. What sport that is not now played at the Olympic Games would you like to see played?

THE GOLD RUSH

What are the men in the picture doing?
Why is the man who is standing smiling?
What is he holding?

It was January 1848. A man was digging near the small village of San Francisco, California. Suddenly, he saw something shiny—gold!

By the next year the California gold rush had begun. Thousands of men came to California. They were called "forty-niners," after the year 1849. The forty-niners came from all around the United States. They even came from other countries, including Mexico, Australia, China, France, and England. They left their families and jobs, and made the difficult trip to California. They all shared a dream. They all wanted to make a fortune in gold.

Towns and camps grew quickly wherever gold was found. These towns were rough places. There was almost always a saloon, where the men drank whiskey and gambled at cards. In mining towns, men stole and sometimes killed for gold.

Did the miners make their fortune? Some did, especially those who came early and were lucky. In 1848, miners usually made about twenty dollars a day. In 1852 miners made about six dollars a day. Many other people came to California to make money from the miners. Prices were very high. A loaf of bread, which cost five cents in New York, cost almost a dollar in San Francisco.

In 1848 San Francisco had been a village. Six years later it was a city with a population of 50,000. In 1850 California had enough people to become a state.

VOCABULARY

What is the meaning of the underlined words? Circle the letter of the correct answer.

1. They all wanted to <u>make a fortune</u> in gold.
   a. make a lot of time
   b. make a lot of money

2. The forty-niners all <u>shared a dream</u>.
   a. had the same dream
   b. wanted a different dream

3. The towns of the Old West were <u>rough places</u>.
   a. places where people fight a lot
   b. places where there are mountains

4. There were many <u>saloons</u> in these western towns.
   a. places to go to drink liquor
   b. places to go to find gold

5. Men <u>gambled at cards</u> in the saloons, too.
   a. played cards to get money
   b. played cards to have fun

6. Some men <u>stole</u> to get gold.
   a. paid for things that other people were selling
   b. took things that belonged to other people

COMPREHENSION

A. Looking for Main Ideas

Circle the letter of the best answer.

1. In 1849 thousands of men came to California because _____ .
   a. they were forty-niners
   b. they wanted to find gold
   c. they had families

2. Towns and camps _____ .
   a. grew quickly
   b. grew where there was a saloon
   c. grew where there was no gold

3. Some of the miners who were lucky _____ .
   a. made twenty dollars
   b. made their fortune
   c. made bread

4. In 1850 California _____ .
   a. had a population of 50,000
   b. became a state
   c. had only one village

B. Looking for Details

One word in each sentence is *not* correct. Cross out the word and write the correct answer above it.

1. In 1848, a miner made two dollars a day.

2. A loaf of bread cost five cents in England.

3. In 1854 California had a population of 500,000.

4. Some of the miners who came late were lucky.

5. Men gambled at whiskey in the saloons.

6. The forty-niners took their families and made the difficult trip to California.

GRAMMAR

Combine the two sentences into one using *and*.

EXAMPLE: Towns grew quickly wherever gold was found. Camps grew quickly wherever gold was found.

Towns and camps grew quickly wherever gold was found.

1. They left their families. They made the difficult trip to California.

2. In the saloons, the men drank whiskey. The men gambled at cards.

3. In the mining towns, men stole for gold. Men sometimes killed for gold.

4. Some of the miners who were early made their fortunes. Some of the miners who were lucky made their fortunes.

5. The forty-niners came from all around the United States. The forty-niners came from other countries.

DISCUSSION

Discuss the answers to these questions with your classmates.

1. California is called the "Golden State." Why do you think it has this nickname?
2. If you lived at the time of the gold rush, would you have joined the forty-niners?
3. How much is gold worth today? Why do you think it is worth so much money?

CHEWING GUM

Unit
7

What do you see in the picture?

Do you chew gum?

We think of chewing gum as a modern American invention. But this is only partly true. For thousands of years people have chewed gum resin, a juice collected from trees. In Mexico, for example, Indians have long chewed chicle, the gum resin from the sapodilla tree.

In 1850 Mexico and the United States fought a war over Texas. General Antonio López de Santa Ana led the Mexican soldiers. When Mexico lost the war, Santa Ana had to leave his country. He went to live in New York and he took with him a large amount of chicle.

An American inventor, Thomas Adams, bought some chicle from Santa Ana. He wanted to make the chicle into rubber but his plan failed. Adams then decided that chicle was better as something to chew. In 1871 he made and sold the first gum balls. These gum balls were a great success.

Then, in the 1890s, a man named William Wrigley first made chewing gum as we know it today. William Wrigley had little education or money, but he had an idea. He made gum into flat sticks and added special flavors. Today, Wrigley's Spearmint gum and Juicy Fruit gum are among the most popular chewing gums in America.

How did modern chewing gum spread from the United States to other countries? During World War I and World War II, the U.S. Army found that chewing gum kept soldiers from getting thirsty. So American soldiers were given chewing gum each day. The soldiers who fought in Europe often gave gum to the people they met. Gum became as popular as it was in the United States. Today, of course, chewing gum can be found around the world.

VOCABULARY

Complete the sentences with one of the following words.

success	modern	spread	led	inventor	flavor

1. When something is up-to-date, it is _____ .

2. The Mexican soldiers followed General Santa Ana's directions during the war. Santa Ana _____ the soldiers.

3. Thomas Adams was an _____ who made chicle into gum balls.

4. Everyone liked the gum balls. They were a great _____ .

5. What _____ ice cream do you like the best—chocolate, vanilla, or strawberry?

6. American soldiers gave gum to people they met in Europe. That is how chewing gum began to _____ all over the world.

COMPREHENSION

A. Looking for Main Ideas

Circle the letter of the best answer.

1. _____ had been chewing chicle for a long time.
   a. Americans
   b. Mexican Indians
   c. People from Texas

2. Thomas Adams _____ .
   a. sold chicle to Santa Ana
   b. made chicle into rubber
   c. made chicle into gum balls

3. In the 1890s William Wrigley _____ .
   a. had no education
   b. gave gum to American soldiers
   c. made gum into flat sticks

B. Looking for Details

Circle T if the sentence is true. Circle F if the sentence is false.

		True	False
1.	American Indians have long chewed chicle.	T	F
2.	General Santa Ana had to leave the United States.	T	F
3.	In 1971 Adams made and sold the first gum balls.	T	F
4.	William Wrigley made Spearmint and Juicy Fruit gum popular.	T	F
5.	William Wrigley had little education or money.	T	F
6.	Chewing gum kept American soldiers from getting hungry.	T	F

GRAMMAR

Complete the sentences with the prepositions below.

from	to	into	around	among

EXAMPLE: Chicle is the gum resin _from_ a tree.

1. Thomas Adams bought some chicle _____ Santa Ana.

2. Adams wanted to make chicle _____ rubber.

3. Modern chewing gum spread _____ the United States _____ other countries.

4. Soldiers gave gum _____ people they met.

5. Spearmint and Juicy Fruit are _____ the most popular chewing gums in America.

6. Today, chewing gum can be found _____ the world.

DISCUSSION

Discuss the answers to these questions with your classmates.

1. Is chewing gum popular in your country? Why or why not?
2. What other American food products have spread around the world?
3. When and where is it not suitable to chew gum? For example, do you chew gum in school, at home, at church, at baseball games?

MARK TWAIN

Who is the man in the picture?

What is he famous for?

Have you ever heard of or read The Adventures of Huckleberry Finn?

Mark Twain, who lived from 1835 to 1910, is one of America's most famous authors. He wrote many books, including *The Adventures of Tom Sawyer* and *The Adventures of Huckleberry Finn*. Mark Twain's own life was interesting enough to be a book.

Twain was born in the state of Missouri, near the Mississippi River. He came from a poor family. His father died when he was twelve, so he had to leave school. While he was still a boy, he worked as a riverboat pilot. He steered boats up and down the long Mississippi River.

The Civil War, which started in 1861, made traveling on the Mississippi impossible. Twain then went west to Nevada. There he worked on a newspaper. In 1864 he went to California to find gold. Twain did not have much luck as a gold miner. He left California to travel in Europe. Twain wrote a book about his trips around Europe.

But the most important influence on Twain and his books was the Mississippi River. When Twain finally settled down, he lived in a house with a porch that looked like the deck of a riverboat. *Huckleberry Finn*, Twain's greatest book, is about the adventures of a boy on the Mississippi River. Another of Twain's books is called *Life on the Mississippi*.

In fact, even the name Mark Twain comes from the Mississippi. Mark Twain's real name was Samuel Langhorne Clemens. On the river Samuel Clemens often heard the boatmen shout "Mark twain!" This meant the water was twelve feet deep. When Samuel Clemens began to write he chose for himself the name Mark Twain.

VOCABULARY

Complete the definitions. Circle the letter of the correct answer.

1. People who write books are called _____ .
   a. states   **b.** trips   **c.** authors

2. The covered entrance area attached to a house is the _____ .
   a. boat   **b.** porch   **c.** luck

3. Someone who looks for coal or gold in the ground is a _____ .
   a. miner   **b.** boatman   **c.** pilot

4. The floor of a ship is called the _____ .
   a. house   **b.** deck   **c.** river

5. The action of driving a ship or car is _____ .
   a. steering   **b.** traveling   **c.** shouting

6. A person who gives directions to help steer a boat is a _____ .
   a. pilot   **b.** boy   **c.** Samuel Clemens

7. When you stop moving from place to place, you _____ .
   a. leave   **b.** come from   **c.** settle down

8. Another word for *trip* is _____ .
   a. influence   **b.** riverboat   **c.** journey

COMPREHENSION

A. Looking for Main Ideas

Circle the letter of the best answer.

1. Mark Twain is _____ .
   a. the name of a riverboat
   b. one of America's most famous authors
   c. the real name of Samuel Langhorne Clemens

2. Mark Twain _____ .
   a. left school to be a writer
   b. was born in Nevada
   c. worked at many different jobs

3. The greatest influence on Mark Twain and his books was _____ .
   a. his poor family
   b. his porch
   c. the Mississippi River

B. Looking for Details

Number the sentences 1 through 10 to show the correct order.

_____ He left school when his father died.

_____ Then he went west to Nevada.

_____ In 1864 he went to California to find gold.

_____ He wrote *Huckleberry Finn.*

_____ Mark Twain was born in Missouri in 1835.

_____ He left California to travel in Europe.

_____ There he worked on a newspaper.

_____ He worked as a riverboat pilot.

_____ Mark Twain died in 1910.

_____ He wrote a book about his trips around Europe.

GRAMMAR

Combine the two sentences into one using *and, but,* or *so*.

EXAMPLE: Mark Twain wrote *The Adventures of Tom Sawyer.* Mark
Twain wrote *The Adventures of Huckleberry Finn.*

*Mark Twain wrote The Adventures of Tom Sawyer
and The Adventures of Huckleberry Finn.*

1. Mark Twain was born in 1835. Mark Twain died in 1910.

2. Mark Twain came from a poor family. When his father died he had
   to leave school.

3. Twain went to California to find gold. He had no luck.

4. Twain had no luck as a gold miner. He went to Europe.

5. Mark Twain was a famous American author. His real name was
   Samuel Langhorne Clemens.

DISCUSSION

Discuss the answers to these questions with your classmates.

1. Who is your favorite author?
2. Why do you think Mark Twain traveled around so much and had so
   many different jobs? Do you think this made him a good writer?
3. If you were an author, what would your books be about? Why?

THE BALD EAGLE

Unit 9

What kind of bird do you see in the picture?
Where do you see pictures of this bird?
Have you ever seen an eagle?

In 1782, soon after the United States won its independence, the bald eagle was chosen as the national bird of the new country. American leaders wanted the eagle to be a symbol of their country because it is a bird of strength and courage. They chose the bald eagle because it was found all over North America and only in North America.

Today, a little over 200 years later, the bald eagle has almost disappeared from the country. In 1972 there were only 3,000 bald eagles in the entire United States. The reason for the bird's decreasing population was pollution, especially pollution of the rivers by pesticides. Pesticides are chemicals used to kill insects and other animals that attack and destroy crops. Unfortunately, rain often washes pesticides into rivers. Pesticides pollute the rivers and poison the fish. Eagles eat these fish and then the eggs eagles lay are not healthy. The eggs have very thin shells and do not hatch. Eagles lay only two or three eggs a year. Because many of the eggs did not hatch and produce more eagles, the number of eagles quickly became smaller.

Today, the American government and the American people are trying to protect the bald eagle. The number of bald eagles is slowly increasing. It now appears that the American national bird will survive, and remain a symbol of strength and courage.

VOCABULARY

What is the meaning of the underlined words? Circle the letter of the correct answer.

1. In 1972 there were only 3,000 bald eagles in the <u>entire</u> United States.
   a. whole
   b. central

2. The reason for the bird's decreasing population was <u>pollution</u>.
   a. other animals
   b. dirty air and water

3. The eggs have thin shells and do not <u>hatch</u>.
   a. open
   b. fly

4. Eagles <u>lay</u> only two or three eggs a year.
   a. eat
   b. produce

5. Pesticides kill animals that attack and destroy <u>crops</u>.
   a. insects
   b. plants

6. It now appears that the American national bird will <u>survive</u>.
   a. live
   b. die

COMPREHENSION

A. Looking for Main Ideas

Write complete answers to these questions.

1. Why was the bald eagle chosen as the symbol of the United States?

   _____

2. Why has the bald eagle almost disappeared from the country?

   _____

3. What are the American government and the American people trying to do for the bald eagle?

   _____

B. Looking for Details

***One* word in each sentence is *not* correct. Cross out the word and write the correct answer above it.**

1. The United States won its independence after 1782.

2. American leaders wanted the eagle to be a sample of their country.

3. They chose the bald eagle because it was found all over South America.

4. Today, a little over 200 years late, the bald eagle has almost disappeared.

5. In 1972 there were only 30,000 bald eagles.

6. Unfortunately, rain often washes crops into rivers.

7. The eagles have very thin shells and do not hatch.

8. Today, the American government and the American people are trying to pollute the bald eagle.

GRAMMAR

Complete the sentences with the article *the*. If no article is necessary, write X.

EXAMPLE: Today *the* bald eagle has almost disappeared from *the* country.

1. They chose _____ bald eagle because it was found all over North America.

2. The reason for _____ bird's decreasing population was _____ pollution.

3. _____ pesticides are _____ chemicals used to kill _____ insects.

4. _____ eagles eat the poisoned fish.

5. Because many of _____ eggs did not hatch and produce more _____

   eagles, _____ number of _____ eagles became smaller.

6. Today, _____ American government and _____ American people

   are trying to protect _____ bald eagle.

DISCUSSION

Discuss the answers to these questions with your classmates.

1. What other countries or states do you know that have animals as symbols?
2. The number of bald eagles became smaller because of pollution. What other animals are growing smaller in number? Do you know why?
3. What causes pollution? What are some things we can do to help stop pollution?

THE AMERICAN COWBOY

What is the man in the picture doing?

What is his job?

Have you ever seen cowboys in the movies?

The cowboy is the hero of many movies. He is, even today, a symbol of courage and adventure. But what was the life of the cowboy really like?

The cowboy's job is clear from the word *cowboy*. Cowboys were men who took care of cows and other cattle. The cattle were in the West and in Texas. People in the cities of the East wanted beef from these cattle. Trains could take the cattle east. But first the cattle had to get to the trains. Part of the cowboy's job was to take the cattle hundreds of miles to the railroad towns.

The trips were called *cattle drives*. A cattle drive usually took several months. Cowboys rode for sixteen hours a day. Because they rode so much, each cowboy brought along about eight horses. A cowboy changed horses several times each day.

The cowboys had to make sure that the cattle arrived safely. Before starting on a drive, the cowboys branded the cattle. They burned a mark on the cattle to show who they belonged to. But these marks didn't stop rustlers, or cattle thieves. Cowboys had to protect the cattle from rustlers. Rustlers made the dangerous trip even more dangerous.

Even though their work was very difficult and dangerous, cowboys did not earn much money. They were paid badly. Yet cowboys liked their way of life. They lived in a wild and open country. They lived a life of adventure and freedom.

VOCABULARY

Complete the definitions. Circle the letter of the correct answer.

1. Cows are a type of _____ .
   a. cowboy   **b.** cattle   **c.** drive

2. When cowboys take a group of cows from one place to another it is called a cattle _____ .
   a. drive   **b.** trip   **c.** train

3. Men who steal cattle are _____ .
   a. cows   **b.** marks   **c.** rustlers

4. When cowboys burned a mark into the cattle, they _____ .
   a. rode them   **b.** branded them   **c.** drove them

5. The cowboy was the most important person in the movie. He was the _____ .
   a. chief   **b.** rustler   **c.** hero

6. The action of taking things or people with you is _____ .
   a. taking care of   **b.** bringing along   **c.** getting to

7. When you are not afraid to do something, you have _____ .
   a. freedom   **b.** courage   **c.** life

8. When you do something new and exciting, you have _____ .
   a. a symbol   **b.** an adventure   **c.** a job

COMPREHENSION

A. Looking for Main Ideas

Circle the letter of the best answer.

1. A cowboy is _____ .
   a. a symbol of courage and adventure
   b. not really a symbol
   c. a symbol of movies

2. The cowboy's job was _____ .
   a. to be a hero
   b. to take care of cattle
   c. to be a rustler

3. Cowboys _____ .
   a. made a lot of money
   b. had a difficult job
   c. did not like their way of life

B. Looking for Details

One word in each sentence is not correct. Cross out the word and write the correct answer above it.

1. Trains took the cattle west.

2. Cowboys rode for eight hours a day.

3. Each cowboy brought along about sixteen horses.

4. A cattle drive took several days.

5. The cowboys burned a mark on the rustlers.

6. The cowboys had to protect the rustlers.

7. People in the East wanted cowboys.

8. Cowboys were paid well.

GRAMMAR

Complete the sentences with the correct article. Use *the* or *a*. If no article is necessary, write X.

EXAMPLE: *The* cowboy is *the* hero of many movies.

1. The cowboy is _____ symbol of courage and adventure.

2. The cattle were in _____ West and in _____ Texas.

3. People in _____ cities of _____ East wanted _____ beef.

4. The cowboy's job is clear from _____ word *cowboy*.

5. Cowboys rode for sixteen hours _____ day.

6. Each cowboy brought along about _____ eight horses.

7. Cowboys burned _____ mark on the cattle to show who they belonged to.

8. Cowboys lived a life of _____ adventure.

DISCUSSION

Discuss the answers to these questions with your classmates.

1. Why do you think the cowboy is a hero in the movies?
2. Are westerns as popular today as they were in the past? Why?
3. Do you like westerns? What other types of movies do you like?

THE WHITE HOUSE

Unit 11

What is the building in the picture?

Where is it?

Who lives there?

In Washington, D.C., 1600 Pennsylvania Avenue is a very special address. It is the address of the White House, the home of the president of the United States.

Originally the White House was gray and was called the Presidential Palace. It was built from 1792 to 1800. At this time, the city of Washington itself was being built. It was to be the nation's new capital city. George Washington, the first president, and Pierre Charles L'Enfant, a French engineer, chose the place for the new city. L'Enfant then planned the city. The president's home was an important part of the plan.

A contest was held to pick a design for the president's home. An architect named James Hoban won. He designed a large three-story house of gray stone.

President Washington never lived in the Presidential Palace. The first president to live there was John Adams, the second president of the United States, and his wife. Mrs. Adams did not really like her new house. In her letters, she often complained about the cold. Fifty fireplaces were not enough to keep the house warm!

In 1812 the United States and Britain went to war. In 1814 the British invaded Washington. They burned many buildings, including the Presidential Palace.

After the war James Hoban, the original architect, partially rebuilt the president's home. To cover the marks of the fire, the building was painted white. Before long it became known as the White House.

The White House is one of the most popular tourist attractions in the United States. Every year more than 1.5 million visitors go through the five rooms that are open to the public.

VOCABULARY

Complete the sentences. Circle the letter of the correct answer.

1. _____ the White House was gray. Now it is white.
   a. Partially
   b. Originally

2. There was a contest to _____ the best design for the home of the president.
   a. plan
   b. pick

3. James Hoban was the _____ who designed the plans for the president's home.
   a. engineer
   b. architect

4. Mrs. Adams _____ about how cold her new home was. She wrote about this problem in her letters.
   a. complained
   b. invaded

5. After the war, not all of the White House needed to be rebuilt, but it did need to be _____ rebuilt.
   a. originally
   b. partially

6. Most of the rooms in the White House are private, but there are five rooms that anyone can visit. These rooms are open to the _____ .
   a. public
   b. popular

COMPREHENSION

A. Looking for Main Ideas

Write complete answers to these questions.

1. Who lives in the White House?

   _____

2. Why was the White House built in Washington?

   _____

3. Why did the original home of the president need to be rebuilt?

   _____

B. Looking for Details

Circle the letter of the best answer.

1. _____ is 1600 Pennsylvania Avenue.
   a. The address of Washington, D.C.
   b. The address of the White House
   c. The original name of the White House

2. The Presidential Palace was _____ .
   a. painted white
   b. made of white stone
   c. made of gray stone

3. The president's home and the city of Washington were _____ .
   a. built by the British
   b. built at the same time
   c. built by the French

4. The first president to live in the Presidential Palace was _____ .
   a. George Washington
   b. Mrs. Adams
   c. John Adams

5. The Presidential Palace was burned down by _____ .
   a. Mrs. John Adams
   b. James Hoban
   c. the British

6. The new presidential home was painted white to _____ .
   a. attract tourists
   b. cover the marks of the fire
   c. please Mrs. John Adams

GRAMMAR

Replace the underlined pronouns in the sentences with the correct nouns or phrases.

The British	Mrs. Adams	The White House
James Hoban	White paint	George Washington
The United States	Britain	Pierre Charles L'Enfant

1. It is the home of the president of the United States.

2. They burned the Presidential Palace.

3. They chose the place for the new city of Washington.

4. She did not like her new house.

5. He entered a contest to design the Presidential Palace.

6. It covered the marks of the fire.

7. He never lived in the Presidential Palace.

8. They went to war in 1812.

DISCUSSION

Discuss the answers to these questions with your classmates.

1. What other famous U.S. buildings can you name?
2. If you had to choose a new capital for the United States, where would you put it?
3. Where does the leader of your country live?

ALEXANDER GRAHAM BELL   Unit 12

What do you see in the picture?

When do you think the telephone was invented?

How did people send messages before the telephone was invented?

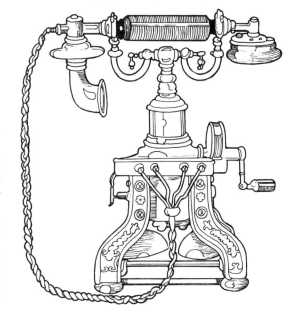

Alexander Graham Bell was born in 1847 in Edinburgh, Scotland. His father was an expert in phonetics, the study of the sounds of languages. As a boy, Alexander became interested in sounds and speech.

In 1870 the Bells decided to emigrate to America. They lived in Boston, where Alexander taught in a school for the deaf. There he began experimenting with a machine to help the deaf hear.

While experimenting with this machine, Bell had an idea. Why not use electricity to send the human voice from one place to another? Bell began work on a new invention.

For years Bell and his assistant, Thomas Watson, worked day and night. They rented rooms in a boardinghouse. Bell was on one floor, and Watson was on another. They tried to send speech through a wire. Finally, on March 19, 1876, Watson heard these words very clearly: "Mr. Watson, come here. I want you." Watson rushed upstairs, ran into Bell's room, and shouted, "I heard you!"

That year was the centennial, or 100th birthday, of the United States. There was a large fair in Philadelphia, called the Centennial Exposition. One of the main attractions at the exposition was Bell's "talking machine." Thousands of visitors, including Don Pedro, the emperor of Brazil, were surprised when they saw—and heard—this invention. But they still thought it was just an interesting toy. They didn't know that one day this talking machine would become the telephone and would change people's lives.

VOCABULARY

Replace the underlined words in the sentences with the words below.

an expert	boardinghouse	the deaf	wire
fair	experiment	attractions	rushed

1. Alexander Graham Bell taught in a school for <u>people who cannot hear</u>.

2. Watson and Bell tried to send speech through a <u>thin piece of metal</u>.

3. In Philadelphia there was a large <u>show where people see new things</u> called the Centennial Exposition.

4. Bell's father was <u>a person who knew a lot about and had training</u> in phonetics.

5. Bell and Watson stayed in a <u>house where there were many rooms to rent</u>.

6. Bell began to <u>try new ideas</u> with a machine to help people who could not hear.

7. One of the <u>interesting things to see</u> at the Centennial Exposition was Bell's "talking machine."

8. When he heard the words, Watson <u>went quickly</u> upstairs, ran into Bell's room and shouted, "I heard you!"

COMPREHENSION

A. Looking for Main Ideas

Circle the letter of the best answer.

1. As a boy, Alexander was interested in sounds and speech because _____ .
   a. he studied phonetics
   b. his father was an expert in phonetics
   c. he was born in Scotland

2. Bell and his assistant Watson _____ .
   a. liked to live in a boardinghouse
   b. could not hear very clearly
   c. tried to send speech through a wire

3. _____ was one of the main attractions at the Centennial Exposition.
   a. Bell's "talking machine"
   b. Don Pedro, the emperor of Brazil
   c. The large fair

B. Looking for Details

Circle T if the sentence is true. Circle F if the sentence is false.

	True	False
1. Alexander taught in a school for the deaf in Boston.	T	F
2. Bell and Watson worked together for years.	T	F
3. Bell and Watson were on the same floor in the boardinghouse in Boston.	T	F
4. Bell rushed upstairs and shouted, "I heard you!"	T	F
5. Don Pedro, the emperor of Brazil, was surprised when he saw the thousands of visitors.	T	F
6. Alexander Graham Bell came to America in 1870.	T	F

GRAMMAR

Complete the sentences with the prepositions below.

through	on	from	in	to

EXAMPLE: Alexander Graham Bell was born ____*in*____ Scotland.

1. Alexander's father was an expert _____ phonetics.

2. The Bells emigrated _____ America.

3. Alexander taught _____ a school for the deaf.

4. Bell was _____ one floor and Watson was _____ another.

5. Bell and Watson tried to send speech _____ a wire.

6. Bell used electricity to send the human voice _____ one place _____ another.

DISCUSSION

Discuss the answers to these questions with your classmates.

1. How do you think the invention of the telephone changed people's lives?
2. How do you think the telephone will change in the future?
3. What kind of invention would you like to work on?

THE JOSHUA TREE

What do you see in the picture?

Where do you think this kind of tree grows?

In the 1840s the Mormons, who are a religious group, traveled west searching for a new home. Many Mormons lived in the state of Illinois. But they had been badly treated and finally were forced to leave. As the Mormons traveled through the desert they became discouraged. Then they saw a strange tree. The tree's branches stretched out like arms. The Mormons thought the tree looked like Joshua, a hero from the Bible. The Mormons thought the arms of the tree were telling them to continue on their way, so they did. They found a new home in the state of Utah. In Utah they saw trees like the one in the desert. They called them "Joshua trees."

The Joshua tree was very useful. The Indians of the West used almost all its parts. They ate not only the fruit of the tree, but also its seeds and white blossoms. They used its leaves for shoes. From its roots they made baskets and colors for clothes.

Settlers in the West used the Joshua tree for firewood and fences. Unfortunately, they often needed to cut down the trees. Some of the trees were as tall as fifty feet. These trees were 700 or 800 years old. The Joshua tree grows very slowly. It grows only about one inch a year.

By the beginning of the 1900s, most Joshua trees had been cut down. People were sad that this strange tree had almost disappeared. In 1936 the Joshua Tree National Monument was established in California. It has many kinds of interesting desert plants, including, of course, many Joshua trees. None of these Joshua trees are fifty feet. But perhaps someday they will be.

VOCABULARY

Which sentences have the same meaning as the sentences from the reading? Circle the letter of the correct answer.

1. The Mormons traveled west searching for a new home.
   a. They were leaving their new home.
   b. They were looking for a new home.

2. The Mormons had been badly treated in Illinois.
   a. Other people in Illinois acted badly toward the Mormons.
   b. Other people in Illinois gave the Mormons gifts.

3. The Mormons became discouraged as they traveled through the desert.
   a. They felt very tired as they traveled through the desert.
   b. They didn't have much hope that they would find a new home.

4. They saw a strange tree.
   a. The tree they saw was unusual.
   b. The tree they saw was useful.

5. Joshua was a hero from the Bible.
   a. There are stories in the Bible about an old man named Joshua.
   b. There are stories in the Bible about a great man named Joshua.

6. The Indians ate not only the fruit of the tree, but also its seeds and white blossoms.
   a. The Indians ate the seeds and the flowers, but not the fruit.
   b. The Indians ate the seeds, flowers, and fruit.

COMPREHENSION

A. Looking for Main Ideas

Write the questions to these answers.

1. Where _____ ?
   The Mormons traveled west in search of a new home.

2. Who _____ ?
   They thought the tree looked like Joshua, a hero from the Bible.

3. What _____ ?
   The Indians used almost all parts of the tree.

B. Looking for Details

One word in each sentence is not correct. Cross out the word and write the correct answer above it.

1. The Indians of the West made shoes from the roots of the Joshua tree.

2. Some of the trees the settlers cut down were 700 feet tall.

3. In Illinois the Mormons saw trees like the one in the desert.

4. The Mormons were asked to leave Illinois.

5. The Joshua tree grows one foot a year.

6. In 1936 the Joshua Tree National Monument in Utah was established.

GRAMMAR

Complete the sentences using the correct tense of the verbs in parentheses. Use either the simple present or the simple past.

EXAMPLE: The Mormons _became_ discouraged.
(become)

1. In the 1840s the Mormons _____ west.
(travel)

2. The Mormons _____ a religious group.
(be)

3. The Joshua Tree National Monument _____ many kinds of desert plants.
(have)

4. The Mormons _____ the tree looked like Joshua.
(think)

5. The Mormons _____ a new home in the state of Utah.
(find)

6. The Joshua tree _____ very slowly.
(grow)

DISCUSSION

Discuss the answers to these questions with your classmates.

1. The Joshua tree was used for many things. What other things can be made from trees?
2. The Joshua tree helped the Mormons and the Indians survive in the desert. How would you survive in the desert?
3. The Joshua tree almost disappeared. What problems are there with the forests of the world today?

THE STATUE OF LIBERTY   Unit 14

What do you see in the picture?

What does the statue have in its hand?

Have you ever visited the Statue of Liberty?

One of the most famous statues in the world stands on an island in New York Harbor. This statue is, of course, the Statue of Liberty. The Statue of Liberty is a woman who holds a torch up high. Visitors can go inside the statue. The statue is so large that as many as twelve people can stand inside the torch. Many more people can stand in other parts of the statue. The statue weighs 225 tons and is 301 feet tall.

The Statue of Liberty was put up in 1886. It was a gift to the United States from the people of France. Over the years France and the United States had a special relationship. In 1776 France helped the American colonies gain independence from England. The French wanted to do something special for the U.S. centennial, its 100th birthday.

Laboulaye was a well-known Frenchman who admired the United States. One night at a dinner in his house, Laboulaye talked about the idea of a gift. Among Laboulaye's guests was the French sculptor Frédéric Auguste Bartholdi. Bartholdi thought of a statue of liberty. He offered to design the statue.

Many people contributed in some way. The French people gave money for the statue. Americans designed and built the pedestal for the statue to stand on. The American people raised money to pay for the pedestal. The French engineer Alexander Eiffel, who was famous for his Eiffel Tower in Paris, figured out how to make the heavy statue stand.

In the years after the statue was put up, many immigrants came to the United States through New York. As they entered New York Harbor, they saw the Statue of Liberty holding up her torch. She symbolized a welcome to a land of freedom.

VOCABULARY

Complete the sentences. Circle the letter of the correct answer.

1. The people of France wanted to give the United States a special _____ .
   a. gift
   b. torch

2. France and the United States had a special _____ .
   a. independence
   b. relationship

3. France helped the American colonies _____ independence.
   a. build
   b. gain

4. A famous Frenchman, Laboulaye, _____ the United States.
   a. admired
   b. visited

5. Frédéric Bartholdi _____ to design the statue.
   a. contributed
   b. offered

6. The Statue of Liberty stands on a _____ .
   a. pedestal
   b. harbor

COMPREHENSION

A. Looking for Main Ideas

Circle the letter of the best answer.

1. The Statue of Liberty is a famous statue in _____ .
   a. France
   b. the United States

2. The Statue of Liberty was a gift _____ .
   a. from the people of France to the United States
   b. from Laboulaye and Eiffel to the United States

3. The Statue of Liberty symbolizes _____ .
   a. a woman with a torch
   b. a land of freedom

B. Looking for Details

Circle T if the sentence is true. Circle F if the sentence is false.

		True	False
1.	Twelve people can stand inside the torch of the Statue of Liberty.	T	F
2.	The United States helped France gain its independence in 1776.	T	F
3.	Alexander Eiffel was among the guests at Laboulaye's house.	T	F
4.	Frédéric Auguste Bartholdi was a French engineer.	T	F
5.	Alexander Eiffel figured out how to make the statue stand.	T	F
6.	Americans designed the pedestal for the statue.	T	F

GRAMMAR

Complete the sentences with the correct article. Use *a* or *the*. If no article is necessary, write *X*.

EXAMPLE: _The_ statue stands on an island in _X_ New York Harbor.

1. _____ Statue of _____ Liberty was _____ gift to _____ United States from _____ people of _____ France.

2. Over _____ years _____ France and _____ United States had _____ special relationship.

3. In _____ 1776 _____ France helped _____ American colonies gain _____ independence from _____ England.

4. _____ French paid for _____ statue.

5. _____ American people paid for _____ pedestal.

DISCUSSION

Discuss the answers to these questions with your classmates.

1. What other famous statues or monuments can you think of?
2. When we think of New York, we think of the Statue of Liberty and the Empire State Building. List five other cities and the buildings, statues, and places they make you think of.
3. Do you have any famous statues or monuments in your country? What are they?

HOLLYWOOD

What are the people in the picture doing?

Who is your favorite actor or actress?

What is your favorite movie?

To many people, the word *Hollywood* has two meanings. Hollywood is an area in Los Angeles. Hollywood is also the American movie industry.

Hollywood was just farmland at the beginning of this century. Early American movies were made in other places; for example, in New York and Chicago.

In 1917 a director was making a movie in Chicago. Because of cold weather, he couldn't finish the movie. He took a trip to southern California, and there he found just the weather and scenery he needed to finish his movie. The director realized that southern California was the perfect place for making movies. The next year his company built a movie studio in Hollywood. Other companies followed. Before long nearly all important American movie studios were in Hollywood, Los Angeles.

The next thirty years were Hollywood's greatest years. Thousands of movies were made, most by a few large and powerful studios. Directors, actors, and writers worked for these studios. They made some movies that today are considered great art.

Hollywood, the area in Los Angeles, also reached its high point in these years. Many famous and glamorous movie stars, like Bette Davis and Clark Gable, lived in Hollywood.

Today, Hollywood is not what it was. More movies are made outside of Hollywood. Many studios have moved. The movie stars have also moved to areas like Beverly Hills and Malibu.

But visitors to Hollywood today can go to the famous Chinese Theater and see the footprints and autographs of movie stars. They can go down the Walk of Fame, on Hollywood Boulevard, and see the golden stars in the sidewalk.

VOCABULARY

Complete the sentences with one of the following words.

glamorous	Nearly	autograph	industry
powerful	scenery	century	

1. Directors, actors, and writers all work in the movie business or

   _____ .

2. One hundred years is a _____ .

3. The mountains, ocean, and trees all make California's _____ beautiful.

4. _____ all the people came to the party. Thirty-six were invited and thirty-two came.

5. The United States is a very _____ country. It has a lot of influence over other countries.

6. The actress looked very _____ in her beautiful dress and diamond jewelry.

7. When a famous person signs his or her name, it is called an

   _____ .

COMPREHENSION

A. Looking for Main Ideas

Circle the letter of the best answer.

1. Hollywood today means two things: _____ .

   a. the movie industry and farmland
   b. farmland and perfect scenery
   c. an area in Los Angeles and the movie industry

2. The great years of Hollywood were _____ .

   a. 1917 and the next year
   b. from 1918 to 1948
   c. after 1948

3. Today, most movies are made _____ .

   a. in Beverly Hills
   b. in Hollywood
   c. outside Hollywood

B. Looking for Details

Circle T if the sentence is true. Circle F if the sentence is false.

		True	False
1.	Some early American movies were made in Chicago and New York.	T	F
2.	In 1917 a director went to California because he had a cold.	T	F
3.	The first movie studio was built in Hollywood in 1918.	T	F
4.	A thousand movies were made in thirty years.	T	F
5.	Some movies are considered great art.	T	F
6.	Today many studios have moved to Beverly Hills and Malibu.	T	F

GRAMMAR

Complete the sentences with the prepositions below.

at	in	to	for	from

EXAMPLE: Famous movie stars like Bette Davis lived ___*in*___ Hollywood.

1. Hollywood means two things _____ many people.

2. Hollywood is an area _____ Los Angeles.

3. Hollywood was farmland _____ the beginning of this century.

4. Some early American movies were made _____ Chicago and New York.

5. His company built a studio _____ Hollywood _____ 1918.

6. Directors and actors worked _____ large studios.

7. Many actors have moved _____ Hollywood _____ Malibu.

8. Visitors can go _____ the Chinese Theater.

DISCUSSION

Discuss the answers to these questions with your classmates.

1. Why were movies so popular in the early days of Hollywood?
2. What has television done to the movie industry?
3. If you could be a famous movie or TV star, who would you like to be?

UNCLE SAM

Who is the man in the picture?

What is he wearing?

Do you think this man is real?

Uncle Sam is a tall, thin man. He's an older man with white hair and a white beard. He often wears a tall hat, a bow tie, and the stars and stripes of the American flag.

Who is this strange-looking man? Would you believe that Uncle Sam is the U.S. government? But why do we call the U.S. government Uncle Sam?

During the War of 1812, the U.S. government hired meat packers to provide meat to the army. One of these meat packers was a man named Samuel Wilson. Samuel was a friendly and fair man. Everyone liked him and called him Uncle Sam.

Sam Wilson stamped the boxes of meat for the army with a large *U.S.*—for *United States*. Some government inspectors came to look over Sam's company. They asked a worker what the *U.S.* on the boxes stood for. As a joke, the worker answered that these letters stood for the name of his boss, Uncle Sam.

The joke spread, and soldiers began saying that their food came from Uncle Sam. Before long, people called all things that came from the government "Uncle Sams." "Uncle Sam" became a nickname for the U.S. government.

Soon there were drawings and cartoons of Uncle Sam in newspapers. In these early pictures, Uncle Sam was a young man. He wore stars and stripes, but his hair was dark and he had no beard. The beard was added when Abraham Lincoln was President. President Lincoln had a beard.

The most famous picture of Uncle Sam is on a poster from World War I. The government needed men to fight in the war. In the poster, a very serious Uncle Sam points his finger and says, "I want YOU for the U.S. Army."

VOCABULARY

Complete the sentences. Circle the letter of the correct answer.

1. The *U.S.* on the boxes _____ *United States*.
   a. stamped
   b. stood for
   c. named

2. "Uncle Sam" became a _____ for the U.S. government.
   a. boss
   b. nickname
   c. picture

3. There's a famous picture of Uncle Sam on a _____ from World War I.
   a. joke
   b. box
   c. poster

4. Sam was a friendly and _____ man.
   a. fair
   b. strange
   c. young

5. The U.S. government _____ meat packers.
   a. liked
   b. hired
   c. called

6. Uncle Sam often wears a tall hat, _____ , and the stars and stripes of the American flag.
   a. dark hair
   b. a bow tie
   c. a box

7. Government inspectors came to _____ Sam's meat-packing company.
   a. ask
   b. stand for
   c. look over

8. Sam was a meat packer who _____ meat to the army.
   a. provided
   b. needed
   c. added

COMPREHENSION

A. Looking for Main Ideas

Circle the letter of the best answer.

1. Everyone called Samuel Wilson _____ .
   a. Uncle Sam
   b. a joke
   c. the United States

2. Uncle Sam is _____ .
   a. the U.S. government
   b. the government meat packers
   c. the name of a government inspector

3. The most famous picture of Uncle Sam is _____ .
   a. on a poster from World War I
   b. in a newspaper from World War I
   c. when he was in the army in World War I

4. In the drawings and cartoons of Uncle Sam _____ .
   a. he wore the stars and stripes
   b. he never had a beard
   c. he had no hair

B. Looking for Details

Circle T if the sentence is true. Circle F if the sentence is false.

True   False

1. Uncle Sam is short and thin.   T   F

2. Sam Wilson was a meat packer.   T   F

3. Everyone liked Sam Wilson.   T   F

4. Sam Wilson stamped the boxes "Uncle Sam."   T   F

5. The government inspectors asked Samuel Wilson what the *U.S.* on the boxes stood for.   T   F

6. "Uncle Sam" became a nickname for President Lincoln.   T   F

GRAMMAR

Complete the sentences with the prepositions below.

with	of	on	in	for

EXAMPLE: Uncle Sam wears the stars and stripes ___*of*___ the American flag.

1. Uncle Sam is tall and thin _____ white hair and a beard.

2. Sam Wilson stamped the boxes _____ meat _____ the army.

3. The *U.S.* _____ the boxes stood for *United States*.

4. "Uncle Sam" became a nickname _____ the U.S. government.

5. There were drawings _____ Uncle Sam _____ newspapers.

6. Uncle Sam was a young man _____ these early pictures.

7. The most famous picture _____ Uncle Sam is _____ a poster from World War I.

8. The government needed men to fight _____ the war.

DISCUSSION

Discuss the answers to these questions with your classmates.

1. What are other symbols that represent the United States?
2. What symbols of other countries do you know?
3. How would you dress today's version of Uncle Sam?

48   UNIT 16

THE CRANBERRY

What do you think is in the can?

Do you think cranberries are sweet or bitter?

When do people eat cranberries?

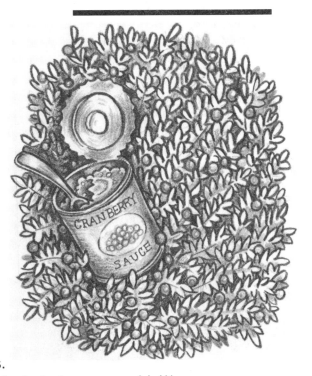

The cranberry is a North American fruit that grows on a bush. The cranberry is small, round, red, and very bitter. American Indians used the berries for food and medicine. When settlers first came from England in the 1600s, they liked these berries, too. The settlers had never seen the berries before. They decided to call them "crane berries," because birds called cranes ate them.

The cranberry bush does not grow everywhere in the United States. In fact, it grows in only five states: Washington, Oregon, Wisconsin, Massachusetts, and New Jersey. These states have the special conditions that the cranberry bush needs.

Cranberries ripen when the weather starts to become cold. We see cranberries in the stores in the fall. Many people eat cranberries as part of the feast of Thanksgiving in November.

Sometimes cranberries are cooked and made into a sauce or a jelly. Cranberries taste less bitter after they are cooked.

Cranberry growers separate the best cranberries from all the rest. It's hard to recognize the best cranberries just by looking. So cranberry growers use a special method, which was developed by accident by a man named John Webb.

One day, as John Webb was taking a container of berries down some steps, he spilled the berries. While he was picking them up he noticed something interesting. The bad berries had stayed on the top steps, and the best berries had bounced down all the way to the bottom. Today, cranberry growers use a seven-step test to separate berries. The best cranberries are the ones that bounce down seven steps!

VOCABULARY

What is the meaning of the underlined words?

1. The cranberry grows on a <u>bush</u>.
   a. a small fruit
   b. a small tree

2. The American Indians used <u>the berries</u> for food.
   a. the fruit
   b. the seeds

3. Cranberries are very <u>bitter</u>.
   a. not sweet
   b. very good

4. Cranberries <u>ripen</u> when the weather starts to become cold.
   a. become ready to eat
   b. become bad

5. The best cranberries are the ones that <u>bounce</u>.
   a. jump up again
   b. do not jump

6. One day, John Webb <u>spilled</u> a container of berries.
   a. carried
   b. dropped

COMPREHENSION

A. Looking for Main Ideas

Write complete answers to these questions.

1. What is a cranberry?

   _____

2. Where does the cranberry bush grow?

   _____

3. Who developed the special method of separating the best cranberries?

   _____

B. Looking for Details

***One* word in each sentence is *not* correct. Cross out the word and write the correct answer above it.**

1. Cranberries taste more bitter after they are cooked.

2. John Webb noticed that the best berries had stayed on the top steps.

3. Cranberry growers use a seven-method test to separate berries.

4. The Indians decided to call the berries "crane berries."

5. Many people eat cranberries at Easter.

6. Cranberries can be cooled and made into a sauce or jelly.

7. Cranberries are in the stores in the summer.

8. It's easy to recognize the best cranberries just by looking.

GRAMMAR

Complete the sentences with the correct article. Use *a* or *the*. If no article is necessary, write *X*.

EXAMPLE: The cranberry grows on __*a*__ bush.

1. American Indians used _____ berries for food and _____ medicine.

2. _____ cranberry bush does not grow everywhere in _____ United States of America.

3. Cranberries ripen when _____ weather starts to become cold.

4. We see _____ cranberries in _____ stores in _____ fall.

5. Many people eat cranberries as part of _____ feast of _____ Thanksgiving in _____ November.

6. Sometimes cranberries are made into _____ sauce or _____ jelly.

7. Cranberry growers separate _____ best cranberries from _____ rest.

8. Cranberry growers use _____ special method developed by _____ man named _____ John Webb.

DISCUSSION

Discuss the answers to these questions with your classmates.

1. What are some of the typical fruits that grow in your country?
2. What foods do you associate with other feasts or holidays you know?
3. What other fruits are commonly eaten as part of a main meal?

THANKSGIVING

Unit 18

What do you see in the picture?

What are they doing?

Do you celebrate Thanksgiving?

On the fourth Thursday in November, in houses around the United States, families get together for a feast, or a large meal. Almost all families eat turkey and cranberry sauce for this meal, and have pumpkin pie for dessert. This feast is part of a very special day, the holiday of Thanksgiving.

In 1620 the Pilgrims made a difficult trip across the ocean from England. They landed in what is now Massachusetts. In England the Pilgrims had not been allowed to freely practice their religion. So they went to the New World in search of religious freedom.

The Pilgrims' first winter was very hard. Almost half the group died of cold, hunger, and disease. But the Indians of Massachusetts taught the Pilgrims to plant corn, to hunt, and to fish. When the next fall came, the Pilgrims had plenty of food. They were thankful and had a feast to give thanks. They invited the Indians to join them. This was the first Thanksgiving.

Thanksgiving became a national holiday many years later because of a woman named Sarah Hale. For forty years Sarah Hale wrote to each president and asked for a holiday of Thanksgiving. At last she was successful. In 1863 President Lincoln declared Thanksgiving a holiday.

How much is Thanksgiving today like the Pilgrims' Thanksgiving? In many ways they are different. For example, historians think that the Pilgrims ate deer, not turkey. The idea of Thanksgiving, though, is very much the same: Thanksgiving is a day on which we celebrate and give thanks.

VOCABULARY

Complete the definitions. Circle the letter of the correct answer.

1. The last part of a meal is called the _____ .
   a. breakfast   **b.** dessert   **c.** lunch

2. When a boat or an airplane has arrived from somewhere we say it has _____ .
   a. feasted   **b.** joined   **c.** landed

3. People who travel from one place to another for religious reasons are _____ .
   a. pilgrims   **b.** families   **c.** Indians

4. When you are sick, you may have a _____ .
   a. hunger   **b.** feast   **c.** disease

5. When you look for animals to kill for food, you _____ .
   a. plant   **b.** hunt   **c.** eat

6. When you have more than you need, you have _____ .
   a. much   **b.** half   **c.** plenty

7. When the government of a country decides to celebrate a special day, it _____ a holiday.
   a. declares   **b.** asks for   **c.** invites

8. People who write history are called _____ .
   a. religious   **b.** historians   **c.** turkeys

COMPREHENSION

A. Looking for Main Ideas

Write the questions for these answers.

1. When _____ ?
   Thanksgiving is celebrated on the fourth Thursday in November.

2. Who _____ ?
   The Pilgrims were religious people from England.

3. Why _____ ?
   They were thankful for food after a hard winter.

B. Looking for Details

Number the sentences 1 through 8 to show the correct order.

_____ The Indians taught the Pilgrims to hunt and plant corn.

_____ In 1863 President Lincoln declared Thanksgiving a holiday.

_____ The Pilgrims left England in search of religious freedom.

_____ Sarah Hale asked every president to make Thanksgiving a national holiday.

_____ In 1620 the Pilgrims landed in Massachusetts.

_____ The Pilgrims invited the Indians to the first Thanksgiving.

_____ The Pilgrims' first winter was hard.

_____ Today, Thanksgiving is a day on which we give thanks.

GRAMMAR

Complete the sentences using the past tense form of the verbs in parentheses.

EXAMPLE: The Indians ___*taught*___ the Pilgrims to fish.
(teach)

1. The Pilgrims _____ in Massachusetts.
(land)

2. The first winter _____ hard for the Pilgrims.
(be)

3. Almost half the Pilgrims _____ during the first winter.
(die)

4. In the fall, the Pilgrims _____ plenty of food.
(have)

5. The Indians _____ the Pilgrims to plant corn.
(teach)

6. The Pilgrims _____ the Indians to join them for a feast.
(invite)

DISCUSSION

Discuss the answers to these questions with your classmates.

1. What other American holidays do you know?
2. What holidays do you have in your country that are not celebrated in the United States?

NOAH WEBSTER

Who is the man in the picture?
What is he famous for?

As a young adult, Noah Webster was a teacher. At this time the colonies were fighting for independence from Britain. Yet the books that American children used in school all came from Britain. The books were all about British people and British places. Webster wanted books that would mean more to American children. So he wrote three books that used American examples—a grammar book, a spelling book, and a reader. These books were very popular, and millions of them were sold.

Webster was interested in changing the spellings of words. He wanted words to be spelled the way they were pronounced. For example, he thought the word *head* should be spelled "hed," and the word *laugh* should be spelled "laf." People liked Webster's suggestions. Unfortunately, though, few words were changed. One group of words that were changed were words in which an unpronounced *u* followed an *o*. That is why Americans write *color* and *labor*, and the British write *colour* and *labour*.

With the money he made from his books, Webster was able to start on his great work. This work took more than twenty years to write. It was the first American English dictionary, published in 1828. Webster's dictionary had over 70,000 words, and gave the meaning and origin of each. To this day, Webster's work is the example that most dictionaries of American English follow.

VOCABULARY

Complete the definitions. Circle the letter of the correct answer.

1. A person that is not a child is _____ .
   a. an adult   **b.** a teacher   **c.** British

2. An idea you share with other people is a _____ .
   a. dictionary   **b.** suggestion   **c.** sentence

3. Sounds that are not spoken are _____ .
   a. definitions   **b.** unpronounced   **c.** spelled

4. The beginning or the start of something is its _____ .
   a. meaning   **b.** spelling   **c.** origin

5. When books are printed they are _____ .
   a. pronounced   **b.** published   **c.** changed

COMPREHENSION

A. Looking for Main Ideas

Write complete answers to these questions.

1. What three books did Noah Webster write for school children?

   _____

2. Why did Webster want to change the spellings of words?

   _____

3. What was Webster's most famous work?

   _____

B. Looking for Details

Circle T if the sentence is true. Circle F if the sentence is false.

	True	False
1. American children used to use British school books.	T	F
2. Webster's books sold 1 million copies.	T	F
3. Webster wanted to change the spelling of words.	T	F
4. The American spelling of the word *color* is different from the British spelling.	T	F
5. Webster's dictionary took exactly twenty years to write.	T	F
6. Webster's dictionary was the first American dictionary.	T	F

	True	False
7. Webster's dictionary had 7,000 words.	T	F
8. Webster's dictionary gave both the meaning and the origin of words.	T	F

GRAMMAR

Replace the underlined pronouns in the sentences with the correct nouns or phrases.

The books	Webster's dictionary	his great work
few words	American children	The British
the money	spellings	Noah Webster

1. He was a teacher.

2. They used British books.

3. They were all about British people and places.

4. Webster tried to change them.

5. Unfortunately, they were changed.

6. They write *colour*.

7. With it, Webster was able to start on it.

8. It is the example for most dictionaries.

DISCUSSION

Discuss the answers to these questions with your classmates.

1. Why is a dictionary useful?
2. Do you think spelling words in American English is difficult? Why or why not?
3. Is spelling difficult in your language? Is it more or less difficult than spelling in English?

SKUNKS, RACCOONS AND COYOTES

Unit 20

Describe the three animals in the picture.

What do you think they eat?

Can you name one special thing about each one?

THE SKUNK

The skunk is known mainly for its bad smell. Skunks are black and white and very furry. They are small—no larger than house cats.

When a skunk is in danger, it attacks by spraying a liquid from under its tail. This liquid has a terrible smell, which may last for many days. A skunk can spray something from as far away as twelve feet.

THE RACCOON

The raccoon is famous for its ringed tail and for the black "mask" around its eyes. Raccoons can use their paws skillfully, and are quite intelligent. They eat many different things— frogs, fish, birds' eggs, fruit, and mice.

Raccoons are not timid or afraid of people. They'll often take food from garbage cans. This explains, some people say, the black masks around their eyes—raccoons are garbage-can robbers!

THE COYOTE

Coyotes are associated with the American Southwest. A coyote howling at night is a familiar scene in western movies. The coyote is a relative of the wolf. Like wolves, coyotes are not popular with farmers because they sometimes kill chickens and sheep. The coyote can live in many different kinds of places. Today, coyotes can be found all over the United States—from Alaska to New York, and in towns as well as in the wild.

VOCABULARY

Which sentences have the same meaning as the sentences from the reading? Circle the letter of the correct answer.

1. Skunks are very furry.
   a. Skunks are very dangerous.
   b. Skunks have a lot of hair.

2. The raccoon is famous for its ringed tail.
   a. The raccoon is known for the black rings around its tail.
   b. The raccoon is known for its round tail.

3. Raccoons use their paws very skillfully.
   a. Raccoons use their heads cleverly.
   b. Raccoons are very good at using their hands and feet for many things.

4. Coyotes are associated with the American Southwest.
   a. When we think of the American Southwest, we think of coyotes.
   b. Coyotes can only live in the American Southwest.

5. A coyote howling at night is a familiar scene in western movies.
   a. It is common to hear a coyote making noise at night in a western movie.
   b. We often see cowboy movies with a coyote walking in the night.

COMPREHENSION

A. Looking for Main Ideas

Circle the letter of the best answer.

1. The skunk is known for _____ .
   a. its color
   b. its bad smell
   c. its fur

2. The raccoon is famous for _____ .
   a. the black "mask" around its eyes and its ringed tail
   b. eating mice and frogs
   c. its paws

3. The coyote is associated with_____ .
   a. the American Southwest
   b. the movies
   c. chickens and sheep

B. Looking for Details

One word in each sentence is _not_ correct. Cross out the word and write the correct answer above it.

1. The skunk attacks by spraying a smell from under its tail.

2. The terrible smell may last for twelve days.

3. The coyote is a relative of the farmer.

4. Coyotes are not popular because they sometimes kill farmers.

5. Raccoons often take food from houses.

6. Skunks are black and white and very popular.

7. Skunks often take food from garbage cans.

8. Raccoons can spray their paws skillfully.

GRAMMAR

Complete the sentences with the prepositions below.

from	under	around	over	in	at	to

EXAMPLE: A raccoon has black rings *around* its tail.

1. A skunk sprays a liquid from _____ its tail.

2. A raccoon has a black "mask" _____ its eyes.

3. Raccoons often take food _____ garbage cans.

4. A coyote howling _____ night is a familiar scene _____ western movies.

5. Coyotes can be found all _____ the United States.

6. Coyotes can be found _____ Alaska _____ New York.

7. Coyotes can be found _____ towns as well as _____ the wild.

8. A skunk can spray something _____ twelve feet away.

DISCUSSION

Discuss the answers to these questions with your classmates.

1. What other animals live in North America?
2. What happens to wild animals when cities get bigger?
3. What things can we do to save animals that are becoming extinct?

THE HAMBURGER

What do you see in the picture?

What do people sometimes put on a hamburger?

What is your favorite food?

The hamburger has no connection to ham. It got its name from the German town of Hamburg, which was famous for its ground steak. German immigrants to the United States introduced the "hamburger steak."

At the St. Louis World's Fair in 1904, hamburger steaks were served on buns for the first time. Hamburgers on buns were convenient and tasted good. This became the usual way of eating hamburgers.

How did the hamburger become the most popular, most typical American food? The introduction of the bun is an important part of the answer. Another important part is McDonald's, the fast-food restaurant.

The first McDonald's was opened in San Bernadino, California, in 1949. Hamburgers were the main item on its menu. People liked the restaurant's fast service. By the 1960s there were many McDonald's restaurants. McDonald's was a part of nearly every community in the United States. There were also other fast-food restaurants that sold hamburgers. McDonald's alone sold millions of hamburgers a year.

Today, of course, there are McDonald's restaurants around the world. The food they serve is considered typically American. And, although McDonald's has expanded its menu, the main item on that menu is—as always—the hamburger.

VOCABULARY

Complete the sentences with one of the following words.

buns	typical	introduction
connection	community	convenient

1. The hamburger is not a type of ham. It has no _____ to ham.

2. Americans first put hamburgers on small, round pieces of bread, or

   _____ .

3. Eating hamburgers on buns is quick and easy. In other words, it's

   _____ .

4. The hamburger is one of the most _____ American foods.

5. The _____ of the bun helped the hamburger become popular.

6. Nearly every city or town in the United States has a McDonald's to

   serve the _____ .

COMPREHENSION

A. Looking for Main Ideas

Circle the letter of the best answer.

1. The hamburger was _____ .
   a. steak imported from Hamburg
   b. a ground steak introduced by immigrants
   c. a convenient bun

2. The American hamburger was different because _____ .
   a. it had nothing to do with ham
   b. it was convenient
   c. it was served on a bun

3. McDonald's restaurants were mainly responsible for _____ .
   a. every community in the United States
   b. the introduction of the bun
   c. the hamburger's popularity

B. Looking for Details

Write complete answers to these questions on a separate sheet of paper.

1. Who introduced the hamburger to the United States?
2. Where was the 1904 World's Fair?
3. How do most people eat hamburgers?
4. What do most people eat at McDonald's?
5. What do you call convenience foods like hamburgers?
6. Why is the hamburger considered a typical American food?

GRAMMAR

Complete the sentences with the prepositions below.

of	on	at	for	By	in	to

EXAMPLE: The hamburger got its name *from* the city of Hamburg.

1. The hamburger has no connection _____ ham.
2. Hamburg was famous _____ its ground steak.
3. Hamburgers _____ buns were introduced _____ the World's Fair.
4. This is the usual way _____ eating hamburgers.
5. Hamburgers were the main item _____ the menu.
6. McDonald's is part _____ nearly every community _____ the United States.
7. _____ the 1960s there were many McDonald's restaurants.

DISCUSSION

Discuss the answers to these questions with your classmates.

1. What types of fast food can you buy?
2. What are the advantages and disadvantages of fast food?
3. What do you think some fast foods of the future might be?

CLARA BARTON

Who is the woman in the picture?

Why is she famous?

Do you know what the Red Cross is?

Some of the early battles of the Civil War were fought near the city of Washington, D.C. A woman named Clara Barton worked in a government office in Washington. When she saw the dead and wounded soldiers, she wanted to help. So she decided to become a nurse. She wanted to go to the battlefields and care for the soldiers.

It was not easy for Clara Barton to become a nurse. Nursing, especially on the battlefields, was considered work for men. Many army doctors did not want to work with women. But Clara Barton didn't listen.

During the five years of the war, Barton helped thousands of men. After one battle, for example, Barton and some of the other nurses spread hay on a hill and helped carry wounded soldiers over to the hay. They carried more than 3,000 men. They then worked through the night, and made bandages for the men who were bleeding.

Besides caring for the soldiers on the battlefields, Barton also traveled around the country getting medicines and supplies. She spoke to important people in the government, and got them to improve conditions in the hospitals.

When the war was over, Clara Barton went to Europe to rest. There she learned about the International Red Cross. The Red Cross helped wounded soldiers and also helped victims of disasters like storms and earthquakes. Barton returned to the United States and convinced the government to join the Red Cross. In 1881 Clara Barton founded the American Red Cross.

VOCABULARY

Which sentences have the same meaning as the sentences from the reading? Circle the letter of the correct answer.

1. Clara Barton wanted to go to the battlefields.
   a. Clara Barton wanted to go to the places where men were fighting.
   b. Clara Barton wanted to go to fight.

2. Nursing was considered work for men.
   a. People thought that only men should be nurses.
   b. People thought that nurses worked only for men.

3. Barton and some of the other nurses spread hay on a hill.
   a. Barton and some other nurses put dry grass on a hill.
   b. Barton said hello to some other nurses on a hill.

4. Barton helped carry wounded soldiers.
   a. Barton helped the soldiers carry those who were dying.
   b. Barton helped carry the soldiers who were hurt.

5. Barton convinced the government to join the Red Cross.
   a. Barton did not want the government to join the Red Cross.
   b. Barton made the American government agree to join the Red Cross.

6. They made bandages for the men who were bleeding.
   a. They made blankets for the wounded men.
   b. They used cloth to cover the wounds of the men who were hurt.

7. Clara Barton founded the American Red Cross.
   a. Clara Barton started the Red Cross in America.
   b. Clara Barton saw the Red Cross in America.

8. The Red Cross helped victims of disasters.
   a. The Red Cross helped people on a hill.
   b. The Red Cross helped people who were hurt in storms and earthquakes.

COMPREHENSION

A. Looking for Main Ideas

Circle the letter of the best answer.

1. Clara Barton wanted to _____ .
   a. fight near Washington
   b. see the wounded soldiers
   c. care for the wounded soldiers

2. During the war, Clara Barton _____ .
   a. spoke to the soldiers
   b. worked for the government
   c. helped thousands of men

3. After Barton returned from Europe _____ .
   a. she rested
   b. she founded the American Red Cross
   c. she helped victims of storms

B. Looking for Details

One word in each sentence is *not* correct. Cross out the word and write the correct answer above it.

1. Clara Barton worked in a government hospital in Washington.

2. Many army doctors did not want to work with soldiers.

3. Barton and some nurses spread bandages on a hill.

4. They carried the wounded soldiers over to the hospital.

5. Barton traveled around the country getting medicines and hay.

6. She got the people in the government to improve conditions in the battlefields.

7. The Red Cross helped supplies of storms and earthquakes.

GRAMMAR

Complete the sentences with the prepositions below.

of	to	around	on	with	in

EXAMPLE: Early battles were fought near the city ___*of*___ Washington.

1. Clara Barton worked _____ a government office _____ Washington.

2. Clara wanted to go _____ the battlefields.

3. Many army doctors did not want to work _____ women.

4. Barton and some nurses spread hay _____ a hill.

5. Barton traveled _____ the country.

6. She spoke to important people _____ the government.

7. The Red Cross helped victims _____ disasters.

DISCUSSION

Discuss the answers to these questions with your classmates.

1. Do you know other famous women in history? Who are they?
2. What are other organizations that help people in trouble?

MOUNT RUSHMORE

What do you see in the picture?
Whose faces are they?
How big do you think they are?

Mount Rushmore is a 6,200-foot mountain in the state of South Dakota. The faces of four American presidents—George Washington, Thomas Jefferson, Abraham Lincoln, and Theodore Roosevelt—are carved into the mountain. These faces, known as the Mount Rushmore National Memorial, are the largest carved figures in the world.

The memorial is the work of the sculptor Gutzon Borglum. The state of South Dakota chose Borglum for the job because he was famous for his huge statues. But, even for Borglum, this memorial was a challenge.

Borglum began work in 1927. The only way to get up the mountain was on foot or on horseback. And Borglum and his helpers had to make the trip hundreds of times just to bring up the equipment they needed.

Borglum had prepared a smaller model of the faces. Points were measured on the model, and then transferred to the mountain to show where to remove rock and how much rock to remove. Workers then used drills and dynamite to remove rock and create the faces. This work was, of course, difficult and dangerous, especially in the cold weather.

The Mount Rushmore Memorial took fourteen years to complete. Borglum died shortly before it was done. His son finished the work. Finally, in 1941, the memorial was opened to the public. People were amazed. The faces of the presidents looked so real, and they were about sixty feet high—as high as a five-story building.

VOCABULARY

Complete the sentences with one of the following words.

sculptor	challenge	carved	statue
memorial	prepare	amazed	equipment

1. When wood or stone is cut by an artist, it is _____ .

2. A _____ keeps the memory of a person or thing alive.

3. A person or animal carved out of wood or stone is a _____ .

4. A person who carves wood or stone is a _____ .

5. Something difficult to do is a _____ .

6. Tools and machines you use to work with are _____ .

7. To make ready is to _____ .

8. If you are very surprised, you are _____ .

COMPREHENSION

A. Looking for Main Ideas

Write complete answers to these questions.

1. What is the Mount Rushmore National Memorial?

_____

2. Who was the sculptor?

_____

3. How long did it take to complete the Mount Rushmore Memorial?

_____

B. Looking for Details

Circle the letter of the best answer.

1. Mount Rushmore is _____ .
   a. a memorial to a sculptor from South Dakota
   b. a 6,200-foot mountain in South Dakota

2. Only the _____ of the presidents are carved into the mountain.
   a. faces
   b. bodies

3. Gutzon Borglum _____ .
   a. was a huge sculptor
   b. sculpted huge figures

4. The faces of the presidents were about _____ .
   a. fourteen feet high
   b. sixty feet high

5. Borglum and his men used _____ .
   a. horses, drills, and dynamite
   b. rock models and cold weather

6. The models Borglum made _____ .
   a. were sixty feet high
   b. showed the helpers what to do

7. Borglum's son _____ .
   a. died before the work was done
   b. finished his father's work

8. The Mount Rushmore National Memorial
   a. is dangerous in cold weather
   b. is as tall as a five-story building

GRAMMAR

Complete the sentences with the prepositions below.

in	of	for	on	up	into

EXAMPLE: Borglum began work _in_ 1927.

1. Mount Rushmore is a mountain _____ South Dakota.

2. The faces _____ four American presidents are carved _____ the mountain.

3. The memorial is the work _____ Gutzon Borglum, who was famous _____ his huge statues.

4. His helpers carried equipment _____ foot and _____ horseback _____ the mountain.

5. They worked _____ fourteen years.

6. The memorial was completed _____ 1941.

DISCUSSION

Discuss the answers to these questions with your classmates.

1. What unusual monuments can you think of?
2. For which famous person would you design a monument, and what would it be?

COCA-COLA

What do you see in the picture?
When did you drink your first Coca-Cola® ?
Where did you drink it?

In 1886 John Pemberton, a druggist in Atlanta, Georgia, made a brown syrup by mixing coca leaves and cola nuts. Pemberton sold the syrup in his drugstore as a medicine to cure all kinds of problems. Pemberton called his all-purpose medicine "Coca-Cola."

When few people bought Coca-Cola, Pemberton sold it to another druggist, Asa Candler. Candler decided to sell Coca-Cola as a soda-fountain drink instead of as a medicine.

At the soda fountains in drugstores, the syrup was mixed with soda water to make the drink Coca-Cola. Candler advertised a lot and sold his syrup to many drugstores. Soon everyone was going to soda fountains and asking for Coca-Cola.

Candler saw no reason for putting Coca-Cola into bottles. But two businessmen thought this would be a good idea. They got permission from Candler, and before long they became millionaires.

As of 1903, coca leaves were no longer used in Coca-Cola. The exact ingredients used and their quantities are not known—the Coca-Cola Company keeps its recipe a secret.

World War I helped make Coca-Cola popular outside the United States. The Coca-Cola Company sent free bottles of the drink to U.S. soldiers fighting in Europe. Coca-Cola became very popular with the soldiers—so popular that the U.S. Army asked the company to start ten factories in Europe. After the war, these factories continued to make Coca-Cola. Today, there are Coca-Cola factories around the world.

VOCABULARY

Complete the sentences. Circle the letter of the correct answer.

1. A person who sells medicines is a _____ .
   a. druggist   **b.** millionaire   **c.** businessman

2. _____ is a sweet, heavy liquid that tastes good.
   a. Syrup   **b.** Cola   **c.** Soda

3. Pemberton sold Coca-Cola to make people well and _____ their problems.
   a. keep   **b.** cure   **c.** mix

4. A medicine that cures many things is _____ .
   a. popular   **b.** all-purpose   **c.** free

5. The different things that are mixed together to make Coca-Cola are its _____ .
   a. ingredients   **b.** ideas   **c.** sodas

6. _____ of ingredients is the amount you put in.
   a. The factory   **b.** The quantity   **c.** The permission

7. Not many people knew about Pemberton's syrup. _____ bought it.
   a. A lot   **b.** Few   **c.** All

8. The way Coca-Cola's ingredients are put together is its _____ .
   a. ingredients   **b.** soda fountain   **c.** recipe

COMPREHENSION

A. Looking for Main Ideas

Write complete answers to these questions.

1. How was Coca-Cola first used?

   _____

2. What did Asa Candler sell Coca-Cola as?

   _____

3. When did Coca-Cola begin to become popular around the world?

   _____

B. Looking for Details

Number the sentences 1 through 8 to show the correct order.

_____ Today, there are Coca-Cola factories around the world.

_____ Few people bought John Pemberton's syrup.

_____ Asa Candler made Coca-Cola into a soda.

_____ That was how Coca-Cola became so popular in the United States.

_____ John Pemberton sold Coca-Cola to Asa Candler.

_____ During World War I, the Coca-Cola Company sent Coca-Cola to U.S. soldiers in Europe.

_____ But two other businessmen put Coca-Cola into bottles.

_____ A druggist, John Pemberton, invented Coca-Cola in 1886.

GRAMMAR

Complete the sentences using the past tense form of the verbs in parentheses.

EXAMPLE: John Pemberton ___*was*___ a druggist in Atlanta, Georgia.
(be)

1. John Pemberton _____ a brown syrup.
(make)

2. He _____ this all-purpose medicine "Coca-Cola."
(call)

3. Few people _____ it.
(buy)

4. He _____ it to Asa Candler.
(sell)

5. Candler _____ it with soda water.
(mix)

6. Two other men _____ permission from Candler to put Coca-Cola in bottles.
(get)

DISCUSSION

Discuss the answers to these questions with your classmates.

1. What other international products can you think of?
2. Why do companies keep recipes secret?

HARRIET BEECHER STOWE
Unit 25

Who is the person in the picture?

What is she famous for?

Have you read or heard of Uncle Tom's Cabin?

Sometimes a book can help change history. One book that certainly did was *Uncle Tom's Cabin*, written by Harriet Beecher Stowe. It was a book that spoke out against slavery.

At the time Harriet Beecher Stowe wrote her novel, there were over 3.5 million slaves in the United States. Slaves were usually in the cotton-growing states of the South. The Northern states had abolished, or gotten rid of, slavery. Yet most Northerners were not strongly against slavery. They were willing to let slavery continue in the South.

Stowe was determined to make people understand that slavery was evil. Each night after putting her six children to bed, she worked on her novel. She told the story of characters like Tom, a courageous old slave, Simon Legree, a cruel man who buys Tom, and Eliza, who makes a dangerous escape to freedom.

Uncle Tom's Cabin was published in 1852. Over 300,000 copies were sold in a year.

People reacted strongly to the novel. In the North, many people were finally convinced that slavery must be ended. In the South, many people were very angry.

Disagreements between the North and the South grew. By 1861 the two sections of the country were at war. The Civil War, which lasted until 1865, finally brought an end to slavery.

Of course, the Civil War had many different causes. Yet *Uncle Tom's Cabin* surely played a part. Stowe met President Lincoln in 1862. As Lincoln took her hand, he said, "So you're the little woman who started the big war."

VOCABULARY

Replace the underlined words in the sentences with the words below.

published	novel	Slaves
spoke out	causes	escape

1. Harriet Beecher Stowe's book <u>protested</u> against slavery.

2. Harriet Beecher Stowe wrote a <u>book that tells a story</u>.

3. <u>People who were not free</u> worked the Southern cotton fields.

4. Some slaves tried to <u>get away</u>.

5. *Uncle Tom's Cabin* was <u>made into a book available to the public</u> in 1852.

6. The American Civil War had many <u>reasons for happening</u>.

COMPREHENSION

A. Looking for Main Ideas

Circle the letter of the best answer.

1. *Uncle Tom's Cabin* was _____ .
   a. a book about Harriet Beecher Stowe.
   b. a book that helped change history.
   c. a history book

2. Harriet Beecher Stowe wanted _____ .
   a. people to understand that slavery was evil.
   b. people to have slaves
   c. slavery to continue in the South

3. *Uncle Tom's Cabin* _____ .
   a. played a part in starting the American Civil War
   b. was written by Abraham Lincoln
   c. told the story of the American Civil War

B. Looking for Details

Circle the letter of the best answer.

1. When Harriet Beecher Stowe wrote her book, there were _____ .
   a. slaves only in the North
   b. 3.5 million slaves in the United States.

2. Harriet Beecher Stowe wrote her book _____ .
   a. after she put her six children to bed
   b. with stories from her six children

3. Before *Uncle Tom's Cabin*, most Northerners _____ .
   a. were slaves in the South
   b. were willing to let slavery continue in the South

4. Harriet Beecher Stowe's book about slavery sold _____ .
   a. 3.5 million copies in one year
   b. over 300,000 copies in one year

5. While many Northerners agreed with Harriet Beecher Stowe, _____ .
   a. many Southerners wanted war
   b. many Southerners were angry

6. The American Civil War lasted _____ .
   a. from 1861 to 1865
   b. from 1852 to 1865

GRAMMAR

Combine the two sentences into one using *and* or *but*.

EXAMPLE: Stowe told the story of Tom, a courageous old slave. Stowe told the story of Simon Legree, a cruel man who buys Tom.

Stowe told the story of Tom, a courageous old slave, and Simon Legree, a cruel man who buys Tom.

1. *Uncle Tom's Cabin* was written by Harriet Beecher Stowe. *Uncle Tom's Cabin* was published in 1852.

2. Slavery had been abolished in the North. Most Northerners were willing to let slavery continue in the South.

3. Harriet Beecher Stowe had six children. Harriet Beecher Stowe wrote every night after she put them to bed.

4. People in the North agreed with *Uncle Tom's Cabin*. People in the South were angry.

5. Disagreements between the North and the South grew. By 1861 there was war.

6. The Civil War lasted until 1865. The Civil War brought an end to slavery.

7. *Uncle Tom's Cabin* did not cause the Civil War. It played a part.

8. President Lincoln took Harriet Beecher Stowe's hand. President Lincoln said, "So you're the little woman who started the big war."

DISCUSSION

Discuss the answers to these questions with your classmates.

1. Do you know any other books that have gotten strong reactions from people? What books have you read that made you react strongly?
2. How many famous black Americans can you name?

JAZZ

What are the people in the picture doing?

What kind of music do you think they are playing? Why?

Can you name some of the instruments?

Americans have contributed to many art forms, but jazz, a type of music, is the only art form that was created in the United States. Jazz was created by black Americans. Many blacks were brought from Africa to America as slaves. The black slaves sang and played the music of their homeland.

Jazz is a mixture of many different kinds of music. It is a combination of the music of West Africa, the work songs the slaves sang, and religious music. Jazz bands formed in the late 1800s. They played in bars and clubs in many towns and cities of the South, especially New Orleans.

New Orleans is an international seaport, and people from all over the world come to New Orleans to hear jazz. Improvisation is an important part of jazz. This means that the musicians make the music up as they go along, or create the music on the spot. This is why a jazz song might sound a little different each time it is played.

Jazz became more and more popular. By the 1920s, jazz was popular all over the United States. By the 1940s, you could not only hear jazz in clubs and bars, but in concert halls as well. Today, people from all over the world play jazz. Jazz musicians from the United States, Asia, Africa, South America, and Europe meet and share their music at festivals on every continent. In this way jazz continues to grow and change.

VOCABULARY

Complete the sentences. Circle the letter of the correct answer.

1. Americans were the first to perform jazz music. It was _____ in the United States.
   a. contributed
   b. created

2. Many ships come to New Orleans because it is a big _____ .
   a. seaport
   b. continent

3. The black slaves sang and played the music of the place they were born. West Africa was their _____ .
   a. combination
   b. homeland

4. When you join with others and give ideas to create something, you _____ to it.
   a. improvise
   b. contribute

5. Jazz musicians from all over the world meet at _____ to play and share their music.
   a. festivals
   b. concert halls

6. Jazz musicians create music as they go along. They invent music _____ .
   a. to grow and change
   b. on the spot

COMPREHENSION

A. Looking for Main Ideas

Write complete answers to these questions.

1. What is jazz?

   _____

2. When did jazz become popular in the United States?

   _____

3. Who plays jazz today?

   _____

B. Looking for Details

One word in each sentence is **not** correct. Cross out the word and write the correct answer above it.

1. Blacks were brought to Africa as slaves.

2. They sang the music of their bands.

3. Jazz festivals formed in the late 1800s.

4. West Africa is an international seaport.

5. Improvisation is an important spot of jazz.

6. Jazz became popular all over the continent.

GRAMMAR

Complete the sentences using the correct tense of the verb in parentheses. Use either the simple present or the simple past.

EXAMPLE: Jazz ___*was*___ created by black Americans.
    (be)

1. Today, jazz _____ to grow and change.
    (continue)

2. Jazz _____ more and more popular.
    (become)

3. The black slaves _____ and _____ the music of
    (sing)   (play)
    their homeland.

4. A jazz song _____ different each time it is played.
    (sound)

5. Today, people from all over the world _____ jazz.
    (play)

6. Jazz _____ a mixture of different kinds of music.
    (be)

DISCUSSION

Discuss the answers to these questions with your classmates.

1. What musical instruments are played in jazz bands?
2. What other types of music do you know?
3. Who is your favorite musician or singer?

GEORGE WASHINGTON

Who is the man in the picture?

Why is he famous?

Where else can you see his picture?

In 1775, when the American War of Independence began, George Washington was chosen to lead the American army. Washington knew his job would be difficult. The army was small. The soldiers were untrained and had few guns. The British army was large and strong. Its soldiers were very well trained.

Early battles showed Washington's problems. His army was easily defeated in the Battle of New York. Then Washington thought of a plan. On Christmas night in 1776, he had his soldiers attack the enemy in the city of Trenton, New Jersey. The enemy soldiers never expected an attack on such a night. They were having a Christmas party. Washington won his first victory. Washington's army won the final battle in Yorktown in 1781.

George Washington was a great leader and was respected by all his men. He was not interested in fame or money, but only in helping his country. There are many stories about George Washington. Many are probably not true. The most famous story, though, is about the cherry tree. It is said that young George cut down his father's cherry tree. When his father asked who cut down the tree, George confessed and said, "I cannot tell a lie."

In 1789 leaders from all the states met to choose the first president of the United States. The vote was unanimous. Everyone voted for George Washington. He became the country's first president, and is remembered as the "Father of our Country."

VOCABULARY

Complete the definitions. Circle the letter of the correct answer.

1. When you admit that you did something wrong, you _____ .
   a. attack   **b.** confess   **c.** lie

2. When you are beaten, you are _____ .
   a. chosen   **b.** voted   **c.** defeated

3. When people have a good opinion of someone else, he or she is _____ .
   a. respected   **b.** strong   **c.** famous

4. When everyone agrees on a decision, the decision is _____ .
   a. large   **b.** unanimous   **c.** true

5. When you have had no practice doing a job, you are _____ .
   a. not interested   **b.** untrained   **c.** cut down

6. When two armies fight, it is called a _____ .
   a. party   **b.** vote   **c.** battle

7. When you are famous or everyone knows you, you have _____ .
   a. fame   **b.** money   **c.** independence

8. When an army wins, it is called a _____ .
   a. plan   **b.** victory   **c.** leader

COMPREHENSION

A. Looking for Main Ideas

Write complete answers to these questions.

1. What was George Washington's job during the War of Independence?

   _____

2. Why did people respect George Washington?

   _____

3. What happened to George Washington in 1789?

   _____

B. Looking for Details

Circle T if the sentence is true. Circle F if the sentence is false.

	True	False
1. George Washington was made president in 1775.	T	F
2. The British army was bigger than the American army.	T	F

		True	False
3.	The British soldiers were better trained than the American soldiers.	T	F
4.	The Americans won all their battles.	T	F
5.	The American soldiers had a party at Christmas in Trenton.	T	F
6.	George Washington was not interested in fame or money.	T	F
7.	George Washington cut down his father's cherry tree.	T	F
8.	George Washington was the first president of the United States.	T	F

GRAMMAR

Complete the sentences using the past tense form of the verbs in parentheses.

EXAMPLE: The American War of Independence ___*began*___ in 1775.
(begin)

1. Washington _____ his job would be difficult.
   (know)

2. Washington's army _____ small.
   (be)

3. The soldiers _____ untrained and _____ few guns.
   (be)   (have)

4. Then Washington _____ of a plan.
   (think)

5. They _____ the enemy on Christmas night.
   (attack)

6. Washington _____ his first victory.
   (win)

7. In 1789 leaders _____ to choose the first president.
   (meet)

8. Everyone _____ for George Washington.
   (vote)

DISCUSSION

Discuss the answers to these questions with your classmates.

1. What other U.S. presidents can you name?
2. What do you know about our present president?
3. What qualities make a great leader?

TORNADOES

What do you see in the picture?

Why is it dangerous?

Have you ever experienced a tornado?

Tornadoes are storms with very strong turning winds and dark clouds. These winds are perhaps the strongest on earth. They reach speeds of 300 miles per hour. The dark clouds are shaped like a funnel—wide at the top and narrow at the bottom. The winds are strongest in the center of the funnel.

Tornadoes are especially common in the United States, but only in certain parts. They occur mainly in the central states.

A hot afternoon in the spring is the most likely time for a tornado. Clouds become dark. There is thunder, lightning, and rain. A cloud forms a funnel and begins to twist. The funnel moves faster and faster. The faster the winds, the louder the noise. Tornadoes always move in a northeastern direction. They never last longer than eight hours.

A tornado's path is narrow, but within that narrow path a tornado can destroy everything. It can smash buildings and rip up trees. Tornadoes can kill people as well.

The worst tornado swept through the states of Missouri, Illinois, and Indiana in 1925, killing 689 people. Modern weather equipment now makes it possible to warn people of tornadoes. People have a much better chance of protecting themselves. But nothing can stop tornadoes from destroying everything in their path.

VOCABULARY

Replace the underlined words in the sentences with the words below.

a funnel	warned	rip up	path
likely	swept	twist	occur

1. A tornado has the shape of <u>something that is wide at the top and narrow at the bottom</u>.

2. A tornado is so strong that it can <u>pull up</u> trees.

3. The most <u>probable</u> time for a tornado is on a hot afternoon in spring.

4. The worst tornado <u>moved quickly and powerfully</u> through Missouri in 1925, killing many people.

5. A cloud forms a funnel and it begins to <u>turn</u>.

6. With modern weather equipment people can be <u>told of something bad before it happens</u>.

7. A tornado's <u>line along which it moves</u> is narrow.

8. Tornadoes <u>happen</u> mainly in the central states.

COMPREHENSION

A. Looking for Main Ideas

Write the questions to these answers.

1. What _____ ?
   They are storms with very strong winds and dark clouds.

2. Where _____ ?
   They are especially common in the central states of the United States.

3. When _____ ?
   The most likely time for a tornado is a hot afternoon in spring.

B. Looking for Details

One word in each sentence is *not* correct. Cross out the word and write the correct answer above it.

1. The winds are strongest in the center of the earth.

2. A tornado always moves in a southeastern direction.

3. A tornado cannot kill people.

4. A tornado never lasts longer than eight days.

5. A tornado can reach speeds of 689 miles per hour.

6. Equipment can stop tornadoes from destroying everything in their path.

7. Clouds become hot in a tornado.

8. A tornado can kill buildings and rip up trees.

GRAMMAR

Combine the two sentences into one using *and* or *but*.

EXAMPLE: Tornadoes are storms with strong turning winds. Tornadoes are storms with dark clouds.

Tornadoes are storms with strong turning winds and dark clouds.

1. The dark clouds are wide at the top. The dark clouds are narrow at the bottom.

2. Tornadoes are common in the United States. They are common only in certain parts of the United States.

3. A cloud forms a funnel. A cloud begins to twist.

4. A tornado's path is narrow. Within that narrow path it can destroy everything.

5. A tornado can smash buildings. A tornado can rip up trees.

DISCUSSION

Discuss the answers to these questions with your classmates.

1. What other types of natural disasters can you name?
2. How can you prepare for natural disasters?
3. Why do you think people rebuild in places where natural disasters occur?

THE TUMBLEWEED

Unit 29

What do you see in the picture?
Have you ever seen a tumbleweed?

Everyone living in the West of the United States knows the tumbleweed. The tumbleweed is just what its name describes. A *weed* is an unwanted plant, and the verb *tumble* means "to roll over and over." When the tumbleweed is dry, the wind breaks it from its roots. It forms into light balls, which are tumbled here and there by the wind.

Most people who know the tumbleweed—especially farmers—don't like it very much. Like other weeds, it grows in with the farmers' crops. Unlike most other weeds, it also grows up fences, in water canals, and in many other places where it doesn't belong. And, unfortunately for the farmers, each tumbleweed plant produces about 200,000 seeds.

Although the tumbleweed is often a nuisance, it can also be useful. Cattle eat tumbleweeds when there hasn't been enough rain for grass to grow. In fact, the tumbleweed is nutritious—it is high in protein, calcium, fiber, and minerals. People can cook the young, green tumbleweed and eat it as a vegetable. Scientists have discovered that we can also burn tumbleweeds to heat our houses. Perhaps the future will find other uses for this unwanted weed of the West.

VOCABULARY

Complete the definitions. Circle the letter of the correct answer.

1. An unwanted plant is a _____ .
   a. crop   **b.** ball   **c.** weed

2. Something that causes problems is a _____ .
   a. seed   **b.** nuisance   **c.** tumbleweed

3. A tumbleweed takes the shape of a ball. It _____ into a ball.
   a. forms   **b.** breaks   **c.** grows up

4. The plants and food that farmers grow are _____ .
   a. grass   **b.** minerals   **c.** crops

5. A food that contains good and healthy things is _____ .
   a. nutritious   **b.** light   **c.** unwanted

COMPREHENSION

A. Looking for Main Ideas

Circle the letter of the best answer.

1. The tumbleweed is _____ .
   a. not what its name describes
   b. not a weed
   c. known by everyone in the West

2. Farmers do not like the tumbleweed because _____ .
   a. it is nutritious
   b. it grows in places where it doesn't belong
   c. it is dry

3. The tumbleweed can be useful _____ .
   a. for scientists in the West
   b. for cattle to eat
   c. for water canals

B. Looking for Details

One word in each sentence is _not_ correct. Cross out the word and write the correct answer above it.

1. When the tumbleweed is young, the wind breaks it from its roots.

2. The tumbleweed grows in with farmers' weeds.

3. Each tumbleweed produces 200,000 roots.

4. People burn the young tumbleweed and eat it.

5. The tumbleweed is light in protein, calcium, fiber, and minerals.

6. The tumbleweed forms into green balls.

7. When there is not enough rain, people eat tumbleweeds.

8. Scientists say we can eat tumbleweeds to heat our houses.

GRAMMAR

Complete the sentences with the prepositions below.

of	in	over	from	into

EXAMPLE: The tumbleweed grows __*in*__ with the farmers' crops.

1. Everyone living _____ the West _____ the United States knows the tumbleweed.

2. The verb *tumble* means to roll _____ and _____ .

3. The wind breaks the tumbleweed _____ its roots.

4. The tumbleweed forms _____ light balls.

5. Protein, calcium, fiber, and minerals are all found _____ the tumbleweed.

DISCUSSION

Discuss the answers to these questions with your classmates.

1. What other plants grow in the desert?
2. What other foods are high in protein, calcium, fiber, and minerals?
3. Besides using plants for food, what other uses do they have?

JESSE OWENS

Who is the man in the picture?

What is he doing?

Do you like athletics?

Jesse Owens was born in Alabama in 1913 to a poor, black family. Even when Jesse was a boy, it was clear that he had special athletic ability. He could run extremely fast. In high school he was a long-jump champion.

Jesse's family didn't have enough money to send him to college. However, because he was an excellent athlete he was able to get a scholarship to Ohio State University. Owens was the star of the Ohio State track team. In one college track event in 1935, he broke three world records in less than an hour! Owens was chosen for the 1936 U.S. Olympic team.

The 1936 Summer Olympics were held in Berlin, Germany. Adolf Hitler had come to power two years before. Hitler believed that the people of Germany and other northern European countries were better than all other people in the world. Hitler wanted to show the world the Germans were the best so he ordered the German team to train hard.

At the Olympics, Jesse Owens won both the 100-meter race and the 200-meter race. His time in the 200-meter race set a new Olympic record. Owens was also on the U.S. 400-meter relay team. The U.S. relay team won.

Then came the long jump. A German athlete broke the Olympic record. Hitler said that he personally would congratulate the winner. But Owens still had one more jump. He jumped several inches further than the German athlete. Hitler left the stadium in anger. Jesse Owens, a black American, had won his fourth gold medal at the Olympics. Jesse Owens was a hero.

VOCABULARY

Complete the sentences. Circle the letter of the correct answer.

1. Jesse Owens got a _____ to Ohio State University.
   a. record
   b. scholarship
   c. champion

2. Jesse was the star of the Ohio State _____ team.
   a. country
   b. meter
   c. track

3. The 1936 Olympics were _____ in Berlin.
   a. left
   b. held
   c. chosen

4. Hitler ordered the German team to _____ hard.
   a. train
   b. relay
   c. win

5. Jesse Owens jumped several inches _____ than the German athlete.
   a. faster
   b. further
   c. lower

6. The U.S. _____ team won.
   a. jump
   b. gold
   c. relay

7. In the 200-meter race, Owens _____ a new Olympic record.
   a. chose
   b. set
   c. won

8. Hitler left the _____ in anger.
   a. American
   b. team
   c. stadium

COMPREHENSION

A. Looking for Main Ideas

Write complete answers to these questions.

1. What special ability did Jesse Owens have?

   _____

2. What did Hitler want to show the world?

   _____

3. How many gold medals did Owens win at the 1936 Olympics?

   _____

B. Looking for Details

Number the sentences 1 through 8 to show the correct order.

_____ He went to Ohio State University.

_____ He went to Berlin in 1936.

_____ Jesse Owens was born in Alabama in 1913.

_____ He was a long-jump champion in high school.

_____ He set an Olympic record for the 200-meter race.

_____ Jesse Owens won the 100- and 200-meter races.

_____ He was chosen for the U.S. Olympic team.

_____ He then won the long jump by several inches.

GRAMMAR

Complete the sentences with the correct article. Use *a, an,* or *the*. If no article is necessary, write X.

EXAMPLE: Hitler ordered *the* German team to train hard.

1. Jesse Owens was born in _____ Alabama.

2. He got _____ scholarship to _____ Ohio State University.

3. Owens was chosen for _____ 1936 U.S. Olympic team.

4. Jesse was _____ excellent athlete.

5. Hitler wanted to show _____ world _____ Germans were _____ best.

6. Hitler said he would congratulate _____ winner.

7. Jesse Owens won his fourth gold medal at _____ Olympics.

8. Jesse Owens was _____ hero.

DISCUSSION

Discuss the answers to these questions with your classmates.

1. What other athletes have won Olympic medals?
2. Do you think athletes should be paid to participate in the Olympics?
3. What Olympic events do you like best? Why?

ANSWER KEY

Unit 1
Vocabulary: **1.** b **2.** c **3.** a
4. b **5.** a **6.** c
Looking for Main Ideas: **1.** What did Americans call frankfurters?
2. Where were dachshund sausages first sold? **3.** Who was Tad Dorgan?
Looking for Details: **1.** F **2.** T
3. F **4.** F **5.** F **6.** T
Grammar: **1.** became **2.** kept
3. got **4.** went **5.** saw **6.** wrote

Unit 2
Vocabulary: **1.** rapidly **2.** apart
3. faced **4.** settlers **5.** trails **6.** tip
7. throughout **8.** solutions
Looking for Main Ideas: **1.** c
2. b **3.** c
Looking for Details: **1.** F **2.** T
3. F **4.** T **5.** T **6.** F
Grammar: **1.** in **2.** to **3.** from, to
4. by, around **5.** throughout **6.** across

Unit 3
Vocabulary: **1.** a **2.** b **3.** a
4. a **5.** b **6.** a **7.** b **8.** a
Looking for Main Ideas: **1.** Levi Strauss came to California to sell canvas to the gold miners. **2.** The miners needed strong pants. **3.** He used a fabric called "denim," which was softer than canvas but just as strong.
Looking for Details: **1.** ~~Germany~~/San Francisco **2.** ~~canvas~~/gold
3. ~~buy~~/sell **4.** ~~clean~~/strong
5. ~~tents~~/pants **6.** ~~Germany~~/France
7. ~~red~~/blue **8.** ~~United States~~/world
Grammar: **1.** Miners **2.** Levi Strauss **3.** canvas **4.** pants **5.** the denim **6.** Levi Strauss

Unit 4
Vocabulary: **1.** a **2.** a **3.** b
4. b **5.** a
Looking for Main Ideas: **1.** c
2. b **3.** a
Looking for Details: **1.** T **2.** F
3. T **4.** F **5.** F **6.** T **7.** F **8.** T
Grammar: **1.** grew up **2.** left
3. went **4.** built **5.** won **6.** cost
7. bought **8.** sold

Unit 5
Vocabulary: **1.** a **2.** c **3.** b **4.** c
5. b **6.** b **7.** a **8.** c
Looking for Main Ideas: **1.** Where did baseball come from? **2.** When did the first professional team start?
3. Who plays in the World Series?
Looking for Details: **1.** F **2.** F
3. T **4.** T **5.** F **6.** T **7.** F **8.** T
Grammar: **1.** X, X **2.** a, a **3.** X
4. a, the, X **5.** X, X **6.** the **7.** the
8. The, the, the

Unit 6
Vocabulary: **1.** b **2.** a **3.** a **4.** a
5. a **6.** b
Looking for Main Ideas: **1.** b
2. a **3.** b **4.** b
Looking for Details: **1.** ~~two~~/twenty
2. ~~England~~/New York **3.** ~~500,000~~/50,000 **4.** ~~late~~/early **5.** ~~whiskey~~/cards **6.** ~~took~~/left
Grammar: **1.** They left their families and made the difficult trip to California. **2.** In the saloons, the men drank whiskey and gambled at cards.
3. In the mining towns, men stole and

sometimes killed for gold. **4.** Some of the miners who were early and lucky made their fortunes. **5.** The forty-niners came from all around the United States and from other countries.

Unit 7
Vocabulary: **1.** modern **2.** led
3. inventor **4.** success **5.** flavor
6. spread
Looking for Main Ideas: **1.** b
2. c **3.** c
Looking for Details: **1.** F **2.** F
3. F **4.** T **5.** T **6.** F
Grammar: **1.** from **2.** into
3. from, to **4.** to **5.** among
6. around

Unit 8
Vocabulary: **1.** c **2.** b **3.** a **4.** b
5. a **6.** a **7.** c **8.** c
Looking for Main Ideas: **1.** b
2. c **3.** c
Looking for Details: 2, 4, 6, 9, 1, 7, 5, 3, 10, 8
Grammar: **1.** Mark Twain was born in 1835 and died in 1910. **2.** Mark Twain came from a poor family, so when his father died he had to leave school. **3.** Twain went to California to find gold but had no luck.
4. Twain had no luck as a gold miner so he went to Europe. **5.** Mark Twain was a famous American author, but his real name was Samuel Langhorne Clemens.

Unit 9
Vocabulary: **1.** a **2.** b **3.** a **4.** b
5. b **6.** a
Looking for Main Ideas: **1.** The bald eagle was chosen as the symbol of the United States because it is a bird of strength and courage, and it was found all over North America.
2. The bald eagle has almost disappeared from the country because of pollution. **3.** The American government and the American people are trying to protect the bald eagle.
Looking for Details: **1.** ~~after~~/before **2.** ~~sample~~/symbol **3.** ~~South~~/North **4.** ~~late~~/later **5.** ~~30,000~~/3,000
6. ~~crops~~/pesticides **7.** ~~eagles~~/eggs
8. ~~pollute~~/protect
Grammar: **1.** the **2.** the, X **3.** X, X, X **4.** X **5.** the, X, the, X **6.** the, the, the

Unit 10
Vocabulary: **1.** b **2.** a **3.** c **4.** b
5. c **6.** b **7.** b **8.** b
Looking for Main Ideas: **1.** a
2. b **3.** b
Looking for Details: **1.** ~~west~~/east
2. ~~eight~~/sixteen **3.** ~~sixteen~~/eight
4. ~~days~~/months **5.** ~~rustlers~~/cattle
6. ~~rustlers~~/cattle **7.** ~~cowboys~~/beef
8. ~~well~~/badly
Grammar: **1.** a **2.** the, X **3.** the, the, X **4.** the **5.** a **6.** X **7.** a **8.** X

Unit 11
Vocabulary: **1.** b **2.** b **3.** b **4.** a
5. b **6.** a
Looking for Main Ideas: **1.** The president of the United States lives in the White House. **2.** The White House was built in Washington because it was to be the nation's capital city. **3.** The original home of

the president needed to be rebuilt because it had burned down.
Looking for Details: **1.** b **2.** c
3. b **4.** c **5.** b **6.** c
Grammar: **1.** The White House **2.** The British **3.** George Washington and Pierre Charles L'Enfant **4.** Mrs. Adams **5.** James Hoban **6.** White paint **7.** George Washington **8.** The United States and Britain

Unit 12
Vocabulary: **1.** the deaf **2.** wire
3. fair **4.** an expert
5. boardinghouse **6.** experiment
7. attractions **8.** rushed
Looking for Main Ideas: **1.** b
2. c **3.** a
Looking for Details: **1.** T **2.** T
3. F **4.** F **5.** F **6.** T
Grammar: **1.** in **2.** to **3.** in
4. on, on **5.** through **6.** from, to

Unit 13
Vocabulary: **1.** b **2.** a **3.** b **4.** a
5. b **6.** b
Looking for Main Ideas: **1.** Where did the Mormons travel in search of a new home? **2.** Who did they think the tree looked like? **3.** What parts of the tree did the Indians use?
Looking for Details: **1.** ~~shoes~~/baskets **2.** ~~700~~/fifty **3.** ~~Illinois~~/Utah
4. ~~asked~~/forced **5.** ~~foot~~/inch
6. ~~Utah~~/California
Grammar: **1.** traveled **2.** are
3. has **4.** thought **5.** found **6.** grows

Unit 14
Vocabulary: **1.** a **2.** b **3.** b **4.** a
5. b **6.** a
Looking for Main Ideas: **1.** b
2. a **3.** b
Looking for Details: **1.** T **2.** F
3. F **4.** F **5.** T **6.** T
Grammar: **1.** The, X, a, the, the, X
2. the, X, the, a **3.** X, X, the, X, X
4. The, the **5.** The, the

Unit 15
Vocabulary: **1.** industry **2.** century
3. scenery **4.** Nearly **5.** powerful
6. glamorous **7.** autograph
Looking for Main Ideas: **1.** c **2.** b
3. c
Looking for Details: **1.** T **2.** F
3. T **4.** F **5.** T **6.** F
Grammar: **1.** to **2.** in **3.** at **4.** in
5. in, in **6.** for **7.** from, to **8.** to

Unit 16
Vocabulary: **1.** b **2.** b **3.** c **4.** a
5. b **6.** b **7.** c **8.** a
Looking for Main Ideas: **1.** a **2.** a
3. a **4.** a
Looking for Details: **1.** F **2.** T
3. T **4.** F **5.** F **6.** F
Grammar: **1.** with **2.** of, for
3. on **4.** for **5.** of, in **6.** in **7.** of, on **8.** in

Unit 17
Vocabulary: **1.** b **2.** a **3.** a **4.** a
5. a **6.** b
Looking for Main Ideas: **1.** A cranberry is a North American fruit that grows on a bush. **2.** The cranberry bush grows in five states:

Washington, Oregon, Wisconsin, Massachusetts, and New Jersey.
3. John Webb developed the special method of separating the cranberries.
Looking for Details: **1.** ~~more~~/less **2.** ~~best~~/bad **3.** ~~method~~/step **4.** ~~Indians~~/settlers **5.** ~~Easter~~/Thanksgiving **6.** ~~cooled~~/cooked **7.** ~~summer~~/fall **8.** ~~easy~~/hard
Grammar: **1.** the, X **2.** The, the **3.** the **4.** X, the, the **5.** the, X, X **6.** a, a **7.** the, the **8.** a, a, X

Unit 18
Vocabulary: **1.** b **2.** c **3.** a **4.** c **5.** b **6.** c **7.** a **8.** b
Looking for Main Ideas: **1.** When is Thanksgiving celebrated? **2.** Who were the Pilgrims? **3.** Why did the Pilgrims have a feast?
Looking for Details: 4, 7, 1, 6, 2, 5, 3, 8
Grammar: **1.** landed **2.** was **3.** died **4.** had **5.** taught **6.** invited

Unit 19
Vocabulary: **1.** a **2.** b **3.** b **4.** c **5.** b
Looking for Main Ideas: **1.** He wrote a grammar book, a spelling book, and a reader. **2.** He wanted words to be spelled the way they were pronounced. **3.** His most famous work was the American English dictionary.
Looking for Details: **1.** T **2.** F **3.** T **4.** T **5.** F **6.** T **7.** F **8.** T
Grammar: **1.** Noah Webster **2.** American children **3.** The books **4.** spellings **5.** few words **6.** The British **7.** the money, his great work **8.** Webster's dictionary

Unit 20
Vocabulary: **1.** b **2.** a **3.** b **4.** a **5.** a
Looking for Main Ideas: **1.** b **2.** a **3.** a
Looking for Details: **1.** ~~smell~~/liquid **2.** ~~twelve~~/many **3.** ~~farmer~~/wolf **4.** ~~farmers~~/chickens and sheep **5.** ~~houses~~/garbage cans **6.** ~~popular~~/furry **7.** ~~Skunks~~/Raccoons **8.** ~~spray~~/use
Grammar: **1.** under **2.** around **3.** from **4.** at, in **5.** over **6.** from, to **7.** in, in **8.** from

Unit 21
Vocabulary: **1.** connection **2.** buns **3.** covenient **4.** typical **5.** introduction **6.** community
Looking for Main Ideas: **1.** b **2.** c **3.** c
Looking for Details: **1.** German immigrants introduced the hamburger to the United States. **2.** The 1904 World's Fair was in St. Louis. **3.** The usual way of eating hamburgers is on a bun. **4.** The main menu item at McDonald's is the hamburger. **5.** Convenience-type food is called "fast" food. **6.** The hamburger is considered typically American because it is one of the most popular foods in the United States.
Grammar: **1.** to **2.** for **3.** on, at **4.** of **5.** on **6.** of, in **7.** By

Unit 22
Vocabulary: **1.** a **2.** a **3.** a **4.** b **5.** b **6.** b **7.** a **8.** b
Looking for Main Ideas: **1.** c **2.** c **3.** b
Looking for Details: **1.** ~~hospital~~/office **2.** ~~soldiers~~/women **3.** ~~bandages~~/hay **4.** ~~hospital~~/hay **5.** ~~hay~~/supplies **6.** ~~battlefields~~/hospitals **7.** ~~supplies~~/victims
Grammar: **1.** in, in **2.** to **3.** with **4.** on **5.** around **6.** in **7.** of

Unit 23
Vocabulary: **1.** carved **2.** memorial **3.** statue **4.** sculptor **5.** challenge **6.** equipment **7.** prepare **8.** amazed
Looking for Main Ideas: **1.** The Mount Rushmore National Memorial is the faces of four American presidents carved into a mountain. **2.** The sculptor was Gutzon Borglum. **3.** It took fourteen years to complete.
Looking for Details: **1.** b **2.** a **3.** b **4.** b **5.** a **6.** b **7.** b **8.** b
Grammar: **1.** in **2.** of, into **3.** of, for **4.** on, on, up **5.** for **6.** in

Unit 24
Vocabulary: **1.** a **2.** a **3.** b **4.** b **5.** a **6.** b **7.** b **8.** c
Looking for Main Ideas: **1.** Coca-Cola was first used as a medicine. **2.** Asa Candler sold Coca-Cola as a soda-fountain drink. **3.** Coca-Cola began to become popular around the world during World War I.
Looking for Details: 8, 2, 4, 6, 3, 7, 5, 1
Grammar: **1.** made **2.** called **3.** bought **4.** sold **5.** mixed **6.** got

Unit 25
Vocabulary: **1.** spoke out **2.** novel **3.** Slaves **4.** escape **5.** published **6.** causes
Looking for Main Ideas: **1.** b **2.** a **3.** a
Looking for Details: **1.** b **2.** a **3.** b **4.** b **5.** b **6.** a
Grammar: **1.** *Uncle Tom's Cabin* was written by Harriet Beecher Stowe and was published in 1852. **2.** Slavery had been abolished in the North, but most Northerners were willing to let slavery continue in the South. **3.** Harriet Beecher Stowe had six children and wrote every night after she put them to bed. **4.** People in the North agreed with *Uncle Tom's Cabin*, but people in the South were angry. **5.** Disagreements between North and South grew, and by 1861 there was war. **6.** The Civil War lasted until 1865 and brought an end to slavery. **7.** *Uncle Tom's Cabin* did not cause the Civil War but it played a part. **8.** President Lincoln took Harriet Beecher Stowe's hand and said, "So you're the little woman who started the big war."

Unit 26
Vocabulary: **1.** b **2.** a **3.** b **4.** b **5.** a **6.** b
Looking for Main Ideas: **1.** Jazz is a type of music. **2.** By the 1920s, jazz was popular all over the United States. **3.** People all over the world play jazz today.
Looking for Details: **1.** ~~Africa~~/America **2.** ~~bands~~/homeland **3.** ~~festivals~~/bands **4.** ~~West Africa~~/New Orleans **5.** ~~spot~~/part **6.** ~~continent~~/world
Grammar: **1.** continues **2.** became **3.** sang, played **4.** sounds **5.** play **6.** is

Unit 27
Vocabulary: **1.** b **2.** c **3.** a **4.** b **5.** b **6.** c **7.** a **8.** b
Looking for Main Ideas: **1.** George Washington was chosen to lead the American army. **2.** People respected George Washington because he was a great leader and was not interested in fame or money, but only in helping his country. **3.** George Washington became the country's first president in 1789.
Looking for Details: **1.** F **2.** T **3.** T **4.** F **5.** F **6.** T **7.** T **8.** T
Grammar: **1.** knew **2.** was **3.** were, had **4.** thought **5.** attacked **6.** won **7.** met **8.** voted

Unit 28
Vocabulary: **1.** a funnel **2.** rip up **3.** likely **4.** swept **5.** twist **6.** warned **7.** path **8.** occur
Looking for Main Ideas: **1.** What are tornadoes? **2.** Where are tornadoes common in the United States? **3.** When is the most likely time for a tornado?
Looking for Details: **1.** ~~earth~~/funnel **2.** ~~southeastern~~/northeastern **3.** ~~cannot~~/can **4.** ~~days~~/hours **5.** ~~689~~/300 **6.** ~~Equipment~~/Nothing **7.** ~~hot~~/dark **8.** ~~kill~~/smash
Grammar: **1.** The dark clouds are wide at the top and narrow at the bottom. **2.** Tornadoes are common in the United States, but only in certain parts. **3.** A cloud forms a funnel and begins to twist. **4.** A tornado's path is narrow, but within that narrow path it can destroy everything. **5.** A tornado can smash buildings and rip up trees.

Unit 29
Vocabulary: **1.** c **2.** b **3.** a **4.** c **5.** a
Looking for Main Ideas: **1.** c **2.** b **3.** b
Looking for Details: **1.** ~~young~~/dry **2.** ~~weeds~~/crops **3.** ~~roots~~/seeds **4.** ~~burn~~/cook **5.** ~~light~~/high **6.** ~~green~~/light **7.** ~~people~~/cattle **8.** ~~eat~~/burn
Grammar: **1.** in, of **2.** over, over **3.** from **4.** into **5.** in

Unit 30
Vocabulary: **1.** b **2.** c **3.** b **4.** a **5.** b **6.** c **7.** b **8.** c
Looking for Main Ideas: **1.** Jesse Owens had athletic ability. **2.** Hitler wanted to show the world the Germans were the best. **3.** Jesse Owens won four gold medals at the 1936 Olympics.
Looking for Details: 3, 5, 1, 2, 7, 6, 4, 8
Grammar: **1.** X **2.** a, X **3.** the **4.** an **5.** the, the, the **6.** the **7.** the **8.** a